THE TREASURE OF KURUKHSTAN

AN ELLEN CHARTERIS INVESTIGATION

JOHN GUTHRIE

Formatting by Robert Harrison

CHAPTER 1

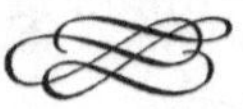

THE VERY PRIVATE DETECTIVE

As soon as she saw the erratic beam of an approaching torch, she knew whose it would be and what he would be thinking.

A light!

At the Dixons' house.

Burgled last night.

Now this.

Well, after all, the constable would be thinking, with a quick glow of excitement, burglars return to the scene of their crime.

Or was that murderers?

She turned off her own light.

The constable saw the light go off and paused. His careful approach had been heard. He adopted the more familiar advance of striding firmly round to the back of the house. He shone his own torch into the blackness, swinging it rapidly round.

As the beam swept round, he saw, as one sees in a flash of lightning, a figure, sitting on a low wall. He slowly brought the torch back round and saw a girl. She seemed not to be aware of him.

He was relieved to find no danger, but annoyed to find no excitement. A girl? What an anti-climax.

"What are you doing?" he said in his sternest voice.

"Thinking."

"Thinking? What do you mean, thinking? Don''t you know that a serious crime was committed here last night."

"That is what I was thinking about," the girl replied. "Have you a key?"

"A key? No, of course not."

"I'd have liked to have a look inside, but it probably isn't necessary."

"Necessary for what?"

"For confirming the identity of the burglars."

The policeman sniffed, in the traditional way, and walked closer to the girl, mainly to confirm that she was just a girl, because she certainly didn't talk like one.

"Do your parents know that you are wandering about at night?"

"My parents have no knowledge of what I am doing. I am down here for a few days with my Aunt. Miss Lomax, at the Shrubbery."

"I know her. Well, does Miss Lomax know that you are wandering about at night?"

"In the first place, I am not wandering about. I came here to investigate. In the second place, no, she doesn't."

"Came here to investigate," the policeman echoed with contempt. "Well, I suggest that you hurry back before you cause a lot of unnecessary worry."

"I doubt that worry is ever necessary. It is just something that people do which achieves nothing. However, Miss Lomax would worry. I had better return to her."

She slipped from the wall, turned on her torch and walked towards the side of the house. "Have you worked it out yet?" she said.

"Worked what out?"

"Who did the burglary."

"Our investigations have begun and will soon put us in a position to know the identity."

"Soon? There are no footprints under the window and the broken glass is outside the window. That's pretty clear I'd say."

"What is?"

"That the couple who look after the house while the Dixons are away committed the crime."

"That the? What the? You stupid girl. Mr and Mrs Kenton have lived in this village for many years and have looked after this house for most of that time."

"My facts are relevant. Yours aren't."

"Now, look here. I suggest that you stop your nonsense and run along and leave this sort of thing to the experts..

"Very well. I'm just trying to help."

"Well, we can manage very well, thank you, without any help from ..."

"Ellen Charteris," was the reply. "And I'm a very private detective."

CHAPTER 2

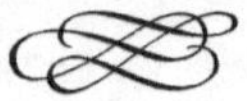

THE NEW GIRL

When Ellen Charteris was introduced as a new pupil, a few days before the end of the summer term, I was mildly interested, just as I was mildly interested in many other things. I saw a tall, rather thin, very serious girl who seemed to be studying every member of the class, as though we were insects in a jar. That was my first impression. Soon, I was to find that it was the right one.

"Ellen is joining at this odd time," Miss Hemmingstall informed us, "because her father, who is a surgeon, recently moved to this area I trust you all to make her feel very welcome. We want her to be as happy to be at St Winifred's as St Winifred's is happy to have her."

Ellen's reply was: "Thank you. I hope that I shall become as fond of St Winifred's as you are of your shoes."

"Er, there's a spare desk next to Joanna Hopewell," said Miss Hemmingstall, rather abruptly. There was usually a space next to me. I wasn't unpopular, and I think my hygiene was as good as anyone else's. Perhaps it was because I was so extremely not extreme in any way. I wasn't particularly *anything*. Not brilliant, but not a dunce. Not athletic, but always willing to have a go. Not head girl material, but not a misbehaver. Mrs Litkin hit the nail on the head when she said that I was a dogged plodder. Miss Campbell was slightly less accurate when she said that I always thought very carefully before doing nothing.

I turned and smiled at the new girl. She didn't smile back. Instead, she regarded me with some intensity, then mild amusement, and said, "I should be interested to know whether you fell over the cat, or the cat tripped you up. Clearly, it doesn't like you."

When I looked surprised, she pointed at the small bruises and scratches on my arms.

At that point, Miss Hemmingstall's stern voice diverted our attention to the lesson.

After a few minutes, Ellen said, "Is she always this dull?"

"Yes," I whispered. "But don't let her see you talking."

Miss Hemmingstall saw *me* talking.

"Jo! Do you have a question?"

"No, thank you, Miss."

"Then did you wish to impart some knowledge?"

"No, Miss."

"Then why were you talking?"

"Er ..."

Ellen intervened. "She was replying to a question which I asked."

"Oh? Then why restrict it to Jo? Why not share it with the whole class?"

"Because I didn't need an answer from the whole class, and I had no wish to interrupt the lesson, which you have now done. I merely enquired of my colleague whether (I flinched and squirmed) this was a typical geography lesson (Some relief; at least she hadn't said 'dull'.)"

"Why? What is wrong with it?"

"I didn't say there is anything wrong with it."

"So, you're happy with the lesson?"

"Not happy. I consider that subjects such as Geography are

taught the wrong way round: outside in, rather than inside out."

"What do you mean?"

"You have been telling us, no doubt in accordance with the curriculum, various interesting facts about a fish which lives several thousand miles away."

"What of it?"

"Round the corner from this school is a fishmonger, called Milsom's. I ask you and the whole class what Mr Milsom is charging for his mackerel today."

No response, except for Miss Hemmingstall's, "You are both impertinent and stupid. What has that to do with this lesson?"

"A great deal. The class is being taught information which will probably never be needed, and which will certainly soon be forgotten, about the habits of a fish several thousand miles away, while knowing nothing about a vital source of sustenance a few steps away."

That did it. The dark cloud over Miss Hemmingstall's face was replaced by a glow of volcanic red. "Report to me at the end of the lesson," she snapped. "In the meantime, sit and listen, and *learn*, and don't say another word unless I ask you to speak."

Lessons never recover from such setbacks. The dark cloud had spread over the class. We wrote and answered questions with a mechanical stiffness. Miss Hemmingstall was not a favourite teacher, but we respected her, and between her and us there was a sort of link, binding the pupils to the teacher. Now, that link seemed to have been broken by this bold intruder.

When the lesson ended, all the girls quickly left the scene of discord and gathered in the yard for the short interval before the next lesson. There was the usual chatter, and a few spontaneous games and some teasing, but I knew I was not the only one who was waiting eagerly for the arrival of Ellen.

When she emerged, the chattering stopped, and there was expectation as Ellen stood on the step. She looked directly at me, but spoke for everyone to hear. "Miss Hemmingstall reminded me that it is only in recent years, and only through the tireless toil of a few people, that young ladies such as we have been permitted to receive a formal education which does not consist mostly of such domestic skills as needlework and embroidery. St Winifred's is not an insipid attempt to provide a bit of academic knowledge: the intention is to prepare girls for professions, provided that marriage and child-bearing don't intervene, which they usually do. But it will never satisfy everyone, and will never attempt to do so. It provides some general knowledge. What we do with that knowledge is entirely up to us, and our circumstances."

After a short pause, she said, "Miss Hemmingstall was quite right to remind me of this. I apologised to her and, quite willingly, I now apologise to the class for disrupting the lesson."

She nodded and left the step. "Oh, by the way," she added, "Four shillings a pound."

I smiled and said, "That was well said."

"It was honest," she replied. "What I said in the lesson was right, but I was wrong to do it in that way."

"Was Miss Hemmingstall satisfied?"

"I think so."

Not quite thinking about it, I said impetuously, "I'll be happy to hear your opinions on matters."

"And I'll be happy to speak them," she said.

And that was how our friendship began. I didn't think of it as friendship, and I knew that Ellen didn't have any such feelings. I was useful, simple, always impressed by what she did and said, and never reluctant to say so. The other girls considered her to be aloof, distant, always putting on airs, and intolerably blunt. In an odd way, those were the characteristics that attracted me. I supposed that we all go through life as someone's, or something's, possession, permanent or temporary. We are someone's daughter, something's pupil, someone's friend, and so on. But all that I seemed to be to Ellen was a person to be observed, studied and analysed.

And I liked it.

If another girl said to me, 'That dress doesn't suit you,' the intention would be to hurt my feelings, and to make me feel inferior. If Ellen said it, the intention would be to provide some information for me. Nothing hurtful; just an observation.

In addition to her personality, Ellen had the disadvantage, in one sense, of being slightly taller than anyone else in the class, except the teacher, and rather lean. That was enough to set her apart. She wasn't *that* tall, and she wasn't *that* thin. But I understood. Most of the other children were short. Their shortness exaggerated Ellen's tallness; and her tallness exaggerated her thinness.

It was that simple.

But most people couldn't work out simple things. And those who could, didn't want to do it.

Ellen always wanted to work things out. Her parents encouraged her desire to know, up to a point. But the constant questions often wore away at their nerves.

"I expect they'd like to be able to send me away to boarding school," Ellen said. "I can see the advantages on both sides, but my father has an excellent microscope, for his studying of insects, and sometimes he lets me use it."

"What do you look at?"

"Anything. It doesn't matter what. It's the detail that appeals to me. The detail of anything.

Of course, things are interesting in themselves, but it's the potential that interests me most. For example, last night, I looked at one of my father's whiskers."

"What? Did you pull it out, or make him put his head on a slide?"

"No. He is a careless shaver. Now, I put the whisker under the microscope and was able to see a small amount of food on the end of it. That might be very important if my mother were to murder him by putting poison in his food."

I was alarmed. "Is that likely?"

"No. It's extremely *un*likely. That's not the point, which is that in such matters, it is the attention to the details that is most important."

"I agree that it's interesting, but I'd prefer it if your example didn't include the possible

murder of your father by your mother."

Such conversations became frequent. That was the basis for our friendship. That *was* our friendship. She told me once that we worked well together because I asked the sensible questions that no-one else would ask, and the silly questions that no-one would ask. By then, I had become familiar with her ways. I was happy to settle for being sensible part of the time. But Ellen said, "No, no. The silly questions are important, too. Without them, it's easy to become bogged down in the clever stuff and miss something which is too obvious."

One day, I asked her what she intended to do with her skills. It was then that she told me about her visit to her Aunt's house and the robbery. It was interesting, but I didn't see it as the answer to my question. I tried again.

Ellen replied, "To be a female private detective, of course."

I laughed. "There's no *of course* about it. In the first place, *are* there such things?"

"Probably not. In which case, I shall be the first, or the only."

I was puzzled again. Ellen said, "You're puzzled again."

I hesitated. "But police work is by recruitment, and all the policemen that I have seen are large men. I don't think they even have women, unless to deal with documents or do the cleaning."

"That is why I shall be a *very* private detective."

"Would they let you?"

"Who?"

"Well, all of them. Your parents. The police. The people in charge. There are restrictions on what a woman may do."

"Well, look at it this way. What are we doing now?"

"Having a discussion."

"A discussion which consists largely of your asking questions and my providing answers."

"Yes."

"Then it could be said that in order to obtain some useful information, you have consulted me."

"Yes."

"And are we breaking the law?"

"No."

"There you have it. People will consult me. In return for my assistance, I might suggest an appropriate donation."

Suddenly, it all seemed ridiculous. Not the plan so much as its being the plan of a schoolgirl in 1886. At St Winifred's, we were given a relatively excellent education, but we weren't expected to use it for anything other than to be competent in any of the roles that were assigned to us. Indeed, it was well known that many men considered any display of education by a woman to be a most undesirable quality. As one eminent gentleman put it, a knowledge of Latin and Greek did not help a woman to sell linen handkerchiefs.

I didn't say any of this to Ellen. Instead, I asked, "When do you intend to start doing this?"

She replied, "I have already begun."

CHAPTER 3

THE MURDER OF LEONARD STINE

The next morning, being a Saturday, I was given permission to accompany Ellen to the home of Mrs Stine, the housekeeper to Ellen's parents, and very recently widowed.

Ellen had shared with me the bit of information that she had. Two nights ago, Mrs Stine's husband, apparently not a nice man, had gone off drinking in the local public houses, and later that night had been pulled from the canal, dead, with evidence of violence.

That was all that was known. Of course, Ellen was very keen to know much more.

The street of small, terraced houses in which Mrs Stine lived was not very pleasant, but you could see that it was respectable. The houses and their front steps all looked scrubbed clean, and there were no menacing loungers under the iron lampposts. There were even some window gardens to bring some cheeriness into the inevitable grime.

As Ellen counted down the houses, a woman washing her window said, "Looking for Mrs Stine?"

"Yes," Ellen replied.

The woman jerked her head to indicate that it was the next house, and said, "Family?"

"Mrs Stine is my parents' housekeeper," Ellen said.

"I'm Mrs Timms. Know about her husband, do you?"

"We know that he's dead."

"No, I mean what he was like when he was alive."

"No," Ellen lied.

"Well, I'm not one to speak ill of the dead, but I'll just warn you that she might not be exhibiting the usual sort of grief."

"Oh?" Ellen was brazenly feigning puzzlement. "Why is that?"

"Well, let's just say he wasn't the most desirable of husbands. I mean behaviour."

"Ah. Inconsiderate."

"That would be a very mild way of putting it."

Without quite shedding her current act, Ellen became more direct. "Please tell me what he did. Mrs Stine has been a loyal and hardworking housekeeper for my family, and I'd like to be prepared before I go in."

Mrs Timms also became more direct. "That night was a typical one, I'd say. He wanted money for booze. I could hear him shouting. Then, the blows. First, his wife, then the poor little girl. Then off he went to, well, as it turned out, one way or another, to drink himself to death."

"So, Mrs Stine might be somewhat relieved that the cause of her suffering has been removed."

"Well, let's just say that *I'd* be pleased if it had happened to me."

"I understand. Thank you, Mrs Timms."

"You're welcome, dear. Give her my love."

We left Mrs Timms cleaning her window.

When Ellen knocked on the door, a voice called, "Come in. It's on the latch."

Inside the small, square room, a woman sat on a threadbare settee. To her right, a girl of about five sat on an armchair of similar quality. As soon as we walked in, the woman rose and exclaimed, "Ellen," with obvious delight. In response, Ellen showed an unexpected warmth.

"Hello, Mrs Stine, and Mary. One pie from mother," she said, holding out her bag. "Two weeks' wages, and mother says come back only when you're ready, and to let her know if you need anything."

Mrs Stine took the bag and started crying. "You're all too kind. I'm very grateful. But I'll be back to work as soon as the funeral's out of the way." Stifling her tears, she added, "Working is good for me."

Ellen said, "This is my friend and colleague, Jo Hopewell."

"Hello, Jo. Any friend of Ellen's is welcome here." She indicated a very threadbare settee and said, "Make yourselves, well, as comfortable as you can, and I'll brew a pot of tea for us all."

I had now started to feel, sense, the delicate changes in Ellen's moods, or rather her performances. She spoke softly and kindly to Mary, but I *knew* that her investigation had begun.

"How are you, Mary?" she asked.

"I am … bearing up," Mary replied. "Thank you for asking."

She was clearly reciting. Ellen glanced at me, and I thought I saw a gleam in her eyes.

"You'll miss your father."

"Yes."

"How is your bruise?"

"Healing well, th …"

"Good," Ellen said, as Mrs Stine came in with two cups of tea.

"The water had recently boiled," she said. "Perhaps you would like some cake."

"No, thank you," Ellen said. "The cake is for you and Mary."

"You're very kind. All of you."

"You are highly valued. Mother often says that she doesn't know what we'd do without you."

A look of modest pleasure was immediately followed by a look of alarm, and Ellen quickly added, "But we can manage for a little while until you are ready to return."

"As soon as the funeral is out of the way."

Ellen changed. Perhaps Mrs Stine didn't notice, but I did.

"Have the police made any progress in finding out what happened?"

"No. Someone saw a struggle, someone fall in the canal, and someone else run off. He, my husband, had a reputation for upsetting people." Emotion was growing, tightening her like the string of an instrument, raising her pitch. "He took the last of my money, leaving us with no money for food, went off drinking, and was killed, and I don't care how it happened, or even who did it, and that's the truth, Ellen, dear. That horrible man is not going to harm us anymore."

She wiped her eyes. "I'm sorry. That isn't the right way to talk about such things to a young lady such as yourself."

"Being the truth, it's exactly the right way to talk to a young lady such as myself. But please excuse me while I walk around briefly. I find it very difficult to keep still for long."

As she talked, she walked round the little room, and into the kitchen, reappearing after a few seconds. "A cosy little house," she said, still looking, listening and sensing. "Just the two rooms upstairs?"

"Yes. My hus …I sleep in one room, and Mary sleeps in the other."

"I do like this house. May I see the bedrooms?"

"Oh, well, not just at the moment, dear. They are not fit for visitors. With all this going on. You understand."

"Of course. And Mary is sleeping in your room now."

"Yes . . . just while she is so upset."

"Of course. And Robert sleeps in her room."

"Er, when he's here."

"Yes. I do like Attar of Roses."

"Ah. You noticed. It's my favourite perfume."

" Also a popular flavour of snuff, popular with people who travel on ships."

"Ah. Is it?"

For a few moments, Ellen looked at Mrs Stine, seeming to fasten her into place with her sharp look. Then she said, "It might be helpful if Robert were to join us."

"Robert? Oh, no. He's . . ."

"Upstairs. He has changed his position twice since we arrived. He provided money for food, he had breakfast with you, and I hope that he will explain why he has been looking in the newspaper at the shipping news."

Mrs Stine looked as though she was about to faint. Mary sat with widely open eyes. I concealed my excitement as well as I could.

Ellen said, "I'm sorry, Mrs Stine. It's . . . my way of doing things. This sad occurrence has many possibilities of explanation. I am interested in the right one. Did Robert kill his father?"

Even I recoiled at the direct question. Mrs Stine drew back and almost shouted, "No!"

"Good. But the police might think so. It is important to ascertain the facts."

Mrs Stine closed her eyes and exhaled loudly. "Mary, ask your brother to come down."

As Mary went upstairs, Mrs Stine said, "Your teas will be cold. I'll top them up."

When she was in the kitchen, Ellen said quietly, "Jo. Please stop disapproving."

"I'm not."

She looked at me in the same penetrative way. "You are

feeling disapproval, and you are shocked. Don't be. It is important to know the truth before the lies and misinterpretations fly about."

Mrs Stine returned with the drinks as Robert came down the stairs. He was tall and very solemn. Suddenly, the little room felt crowded with people and emotion.

We stood as Mrs Stine said, "Robert, this is my employer's daughter, Ellen, and her friend, Jo. Ellen has been, well, taking an interest in our little tragedy."

"Hello, Robert," Ellen said, shaking his hand. "Please excuse my bluntness, all of you. My friend and I brought some things from my parents, including reassurances. That was the reason for our visit. However, I added to that my curiosity concerning the death of your father, and my desire to know the truth about it. It is a special interest of mine, in the pursuit of which it is necessary for me to be somewhat detached from circulating emotions. It is not my wish to cause offence by doing so."

Robert said, "You are a very unusual girl."

Was that a whimsical look that I saw? "You are right, Robert. I *am* very unusual. And I believe that this event is very unusual."

Robert shrugged. "The most unusual thing is that it hasn't happened before. For years, he has been extremely cruel to my mother, and to little Mary. It is a terrible thing to say, that by his death, a great sorrow, and a great dread, have been lifted from us."

"So you are glad that he is dead."

"For the sake of my mother and my sister, yes, I am glad." He hesitated, then said, "By that I do not mean that I hate him, or wish him harm in whatever place or state he is now; I mean that I am glad there is now an end to the suffering of my mother and sister at his hands. To modify my earlier response, it is his removal, rather than his death, for which I am glad. I should have been happy for him to have gone to live thousands of miles away. That would have been satisfactory for achieving the same result that this has."

"Thank you, Robert. I understand that. Not through experience, but through your honest eloquence. Before you joined us, I asked your mother whether you killed your father. She answered that you had not. Were you in any way involved in his death?"

There was a moment of hesitation before he answered, "Not directly, no."

"I suspect that your *in*direct involvement has many connecting strands. Are you willing to provide the information for me?"

He gave a little sigh and said, "Yes. It is long and complicated. There is danger to me, and I am determined that this danger will not affect my family. Or, indeed, you and your friend. I must not stay here. I must return to Kurukhstan urgently in order to put something right, which, perhaps, I have inadvertently put wrong. But I can't go there yet, because I don't have the means to put the thing right. I must find somewhere to hide while I sort out this mess. I must go out of your lives. But first, I am writing my account, with instructions, intending to leave it to be read in my absence, or … in the event of anything worse happening."

Mrs Stine rubbed her temples and said, "One thing after another. One burden is removed, and another one appears."

He reached to her and squeezed her arm. "I shall do my best to prevent its being a burden on you and Mary. That is my most earnest wish."

He turned to Ellen, and, politely, to me. "You girls had better return to your homes. I must do what I can to put things right. In the meantime, I shall finish my account, which I hope will protect all of you."

Ellen stared in thought for a few moments, then said, "Yes, your mother and sister must be protected. However, the safety of me, and my associate, is not be considered. We are the investigators of this crime, and must accept the dangers from it."

As Robert opened his mouth to object, she said, "But you are right about our returning home. We are still subject to our own domestic protection and regulations, especially Jo; and the more that we stretch the flexible restrictions, the more likely we are to be further restricted. We shall return as soon as we may. Please take good care. People see and hear, whether or not they intend to do so."

Mrs Stine said, "Yes. It is very difficult to keep things secret here; small houses, thin walls, neighbours who stand or sit on steps, many of them out of work and nothing better to do ...."

"Neighbours cleaning windows," suggested Ellen.

Mrs Stine smiled. She understood the reference."

"Then, take care," Ellen said. "Even without bad intentions, people talk. And talk spreads, and is often heard by the wrong people."

Looking at Mrs Stine and her son, I could see that they had taken the step that I had done, no longer thinking of Ellen as a child. Her comments, including her advice, had no precociousness, but were accepted as the sort of sensible advice that might come from a wise and experienced adult.

After that, we took our leave, with warmth mixed with the formality that the circumstances, and Ellen's manner, imposed on us.

When we were walking home, Ellen said, "These home and school restrictions are extremely inconvenient. I need to be thinking about the crime, which I can't do usefully until I have Robert's account, and when school has stretched its influence into the holiday, with books to be read and essays to be written."

She turned to me, her eyes ablaze, and said with unexpected passion, "I don't have the time, Jo, or the interest, when there are important things to do." She held up a placatory hand. "Yes, I know how important books and learning are. Of course I do. But I must focus completely on this case. You know what obstacles there are for me because you stated them. Therefore, thought, research, and plain meticulous observation are vital. I *must* succeed, Jo. For the Stines, for the rightness of the thing, and for *me*. Yes, for me."

I said, "I understand." And I did. She gave one quick nod and sealed her emotions up again.

Trying to contribute, I said, "As it stands, there are too many suspects."

"Exactly. A violent and hated man is killed. Whom do you suspect? There could be a hundred possible people. I need that account by Robert; and then, Jo, I suspect we shall be at the *beginning* of the investigation."

CHAPTER 4

AN INTERLUDE IN THE PARK

For my family, Sundays were in an inflexible routine. A light breakfast was followed by the social gathering at our local church. Reflecting our social position and taste in all things, it was not high or low, and never controversial. The Reverend Smithson always reminded us of the constant proximity of wickedness and the need to be vigilant. A woman in a large hat on the front row always turned and looked in a general way at the congregation, as though to say, 'He means you.'

After lunch, on fine days, we went to the Park. My father always enjoyed this. On that Sunday, he was particularly effusive. "Look at it," he said. "Not a trouble-maker to be seen. Middle class and working class, bankers, soldiers, nannies, mill hands, all taking the air, enjoying the greenery, listening to the band. This is how it ought to be."

Although, through hard work and conscientiousness, my father believed that he was now firmly in the middle class, he was not ashamed to admit that his origins lay well below that level. Although he disapproved of all violent, or even aggressive, agitation, and always had little sympathy for those who wanted more money, he also disapproved of the treatment of the working classes as inferiors and potential rioters, to be kept at their work, or at least out of the locked parks, on Sunday afternoons.

It was a beautiful park, and I trust still is. An excellent place to take the air and look at the flowers and the ducks. As we walked slowly through the rose garden, we could still hear the jolly melodies from the bandstand. This seemed to be another country from where Mrs Stine and Mary lived, where the cramped little houses gasped for air, where the dark water of the canal bore barges and filth in similarly sluggish progress.

But whereas even a few days ago, my walk would have been accompanied by no alertness of thought, I now became aware of the Ellen effect. Bees buzz because they are working hard, the sun does not really go down, *and wouldn't a dirty canal be a good place in which to hide the weapon which killed Leonard Stine*?

I knew that even if the weapon were in the canal, it would probably stay there, hidden in the thick water, mud and many other items which would be on the canal bed. What was exciting was my having had the thought. On this sunny day, in this beautiful park, I was thinking darkly as the criminal might have done. To keep the weapon as he fled would be to risk being caught with it or having the problem of finding somewhere to hide it. If I had committed the crime, I'd want to have nothing more to do with the weapon. I'd fling it out into the middle of the canal, where, even if it were found one day, it could not be identified as the murder weapon, and could not be proved to have been used by me.

I was thinking as the criminal might have done.

I wanted to slap my own face and shake myself and remind myself that I was Jo Hopewell, a simple and rather dull schoolgirl. Instead, I looked around, noticing details in the flowers and shrubs, and the people passing by. They were no longer mere peripheral characters in my daily life; they were little parcels of potential or hidden drama, each one capable of plotting or losing control for a vital moment; of deceiving, of luring, of stealing, of being the victim of any one of these.

I became aware that I was bending down, leaning over a flower. It was no longer just a thing of pretty petals: now I saw the whole thing, petals, stigma, stamen. As a bee descended, I saw the vital link between the flower, showing its colours not to be pretty for arrogant humans, who think that everything is done for their benefit, but in order to attract the bee, which collected the pollen and rubbed that pollen against other plants, ensuring the continuation of the plants.

Everything fitting together, parts of the whole, *all in the details*.

"Excellent."

I turned, startled, to find Ellen beside me. She shrugged and said, "My parents had the same idea, and contrary to what you might think of me, I like nothing better than to stroll in the park with my parents."

Our parents were doing introductions. Ellen's father was a large, stocky man with a large beard. Her mother was tall and slender. Both seemed very sure of themselves, and I knew that my parents would be struggling with their innate shyness and lack of confidence outside their usual social routines.

I said to Ellen, "In that case, we have probably passed many times."

"Yes, we have."

I sighed. "I didn't notice. I'm not an observant person. I tend to daydream or look about me vaguely."

"Ah, but I saw an improvement a few moments ago," Ellen said. "You *were* observing. Before you met me, your description of this park would have been all about the flowers and shrubs and trees, concentrating on their colours. Now, you see much more, and I was impressed by your watching the people who were passing. It's a beginning. The beginning of noticing, of observing. Learn to remember what you see. Store your observations in various sections of your brain. Like a library. When something is needed, you go to the right section and remove the information to be used."

"Oh, Ellen. I'll do my best, but I'll never be like you."

"Of course you won't. Don't ever try. Be *you*. But be a better you. A you who is going to be so helpful to me."

I laughed. "Well, that is a nice ambition to have."

"And a very worthwhile one."

There was no smile, but her eyes sparkled like night stars. There was plenty of merriment inside Ellen Charteris, but she made sure that it stayed there.

I told her about the possibility that the killer threw the weapon into the canal. "Yes," she agreed. "It is the obvious place. As soon as we arrived, I tried to think of a way of searching, but you are probably right. There must be a lot of items at the bottom, most of them suitable murder weapons."

I was a little disappointed because I had so recently had what I thought was an inspired thought. Perhaps she saw this, because she said, "But that's what we need: lots of thinking and imagining. The important thing is to think that the murder weapon might be in the canal, but then to think, well, what if it weren't? Where might it be?"

The deep voice of Ellen's father penetrated the intensity of our conversation. My lesson. "Ellen. Are you turning that poor girl's head and leading her into your own morbid ways."

"I am encouraging her to be observant, Father. As you are with your microscope."

As he turned back to my parents, I thought that I saw that same sparkle in the eyes. He seemed to have enjoyed the exchange with his daughter, which was not the usual response when a daughter gave a neat reply to her father.

There was sombre discussion about the recent murder, and both Ellen and I listened. Ellen's parents said that they would attend the funeral in order to provide support for Mrs Stine, but that it wouldn't be in any way a social occasion.

"Understandably," said Dr Charteris, "the poor woman wants it done and out of the way. She is looking forward to resuming her work with us, and we shall ensure that she is always financially secure."

Ellen boldly took the opportunity to suggest that she and I go to the house and take care of Mary during the funeral. Her father replied, "Provided that Mrs Stine is happy with that arrangement, I don't that we could reasonably object."

My parents neither approved nor objected, reduced by circumstances and Dr Charteris's forecful personality to being observers rather than active participators.

Shortly after that, there was the customary passing of cards and addresses, and promises to visit, Ellen and I parted, and our two families went their slightly separate ways.

"Very nice people," said Father.

"Very interesting," said Mother, somehow making the adjective sound slightly undesirable, as though Mr and Mrs Charteris had just performed some acrobatic manoeuvres.

"So that's your little friend," Father said.

I ignored the all-round inappropriateness of 'little' and replied, "Yes."

"Hmm."

I knew what he was thinking: that when Mr Charteris asked his question, Ellen should have replied, 'No, Father' or 'Yes, Father. I'm sorry.'

"She seems rather adult in her ways."

I plunged in, saying warmly, "Yes, she is very mature and sensible. Just the sort of friend that I need."

"Yes, yes. But don't forget that you *are* still a child, no matter what she might think."

"Yes, Father." I knew that defending Ellen would be seen as an example of her bad influence. By 'child', Father was not referring to the retention of innocence, but to the retention of obedience. He had no desire to be oppressive, but he wanted everything in his life to proceed in an orderly, predictable manner, enabling him to be fully in control.

I must admit that rather a lot of that had rubbed off *on* me; now, Ellen was busily and effectively rubbing it *off* me.

CHAPTER 5

A VISIT FROM PATRICK STINE

Mrs Stine was very pleased that we were going to take care of Mary during the funeral. Ellen's mother had brought some food, but insisted that it was for Mrs Stine and Mary.

Even for normal funerals," she said, "I don't approve of turning them into gluttonous parties. I am sure that you will want some quiet time to yourselves afterwards."

She looked at Ellen and me, her meaning clear.

Ellen responded with, "As soon as Mrs Stine is ready to be left alone, we shall of course comply."

"Yes, dear," Mrs Charteris replied very smoothly. "But please ensure that the interpretation of when she is ready is Mrs Stine's, not yours."

"Yes, of course, mother."

I had the clear impression that there was a good-natured duel taking place.

As soon as the three adults had left, Ellen and I did our best to distract Mary with some simple games in a corner of the room, beneath the stairs. The poor girl had very little, and showed little interest. Ellen did her best to join in, but there was the usual remoteness. She was thinking, and, as always, observing. And listening. I did my best with Mary, but with two remote, detached people with me, it wasn't easy.

It wasn't long before we heard the creak of the stairs. "Hello, again," Robert said, trying to be cheerful.

"Hello, Robert," we both replied, and Ellen added, "Have you finished the account?"

"I think so."

He gave Mary a cuddle and headed for the kitchen. I noticed Ellen stiffen, and turn to look at the front door.

It was slowly opening.

A man took two steps into the room. He sneered and nodded his head as though to confirm what he had suspected. He spoke ominously.

"Hello, Robert. I did think you might be here. No doubt, you'd have liked to be at the funeral, but of course that wouldn't be advisable."

"Uncle Patrick. Cast in the same mould as my father."

"Come now, nephew. You dear father is dead. Show some respect."

"His death was not an accomplishment, and did nothing to expunge his horrible treatment of my mother."

"But was that an acceptable reason for killing him? Or was there, perhaps, another reason. Eh, Robert?"

"What do you want?"

"What do I want? I want payment, Robert. Payment for not telling the police what I know about what happened by the canal, payment for not telling them *why* it happened, for not telling them about something valuable which Len had. Probably stolen from you. Am I right? Am I close?"

"I have nothing to say to you, other than that I won't pay you anything."

"Not even to keep me from telling the police what I know?"

"No! Tell *what* you want, to *whom* you want. I will pay you nothing."

"I'll give you a few hours to think it over. Then, I'll go to the police."

"What would going to the police gain for you?"

"Look, Robert. I'm not asking for a lot. I need some cash right now for business purposes. Just to set me straight for a few days until I start making some big profits. You'll have my word that I shan't tell the police what I witnessed."

"Patrick! I did not kill my father! Quite apart from all the other objections, it would be absurd to pay someone to tell the truth."

"But what if it appears, based on my witness statement, that you *did* kill your father?"

"Are you the witness?"

Ellen's question made him flinch. As he turned to look at Ellen, the question seemed to hang in the air. Looking back at Robert, he nodded towards Ellen and said, "Who's she?"

Robert hesitated, but only because he didn't know how to answer the question in a simple manner. Ellen said, "I am a friend of the family. So is my friend here. And the reason for my question is that as the principal witness, your ability to observe is rather important. You didn't see three children across the room. How far away were you from the scene which you have described? It was in the darkness of night, wasn't it?"

"Are these some sort of defence witnesses?" was the evasive response.

"As she said, they are friends of mine. Please treat them with respect."

"Respect? This one's asking for a thrashing."

Ellen said, "Don't worry, Robert. He has no credibility as a witness, and no self-control to deal with examination in a courtroom."

The enraged man took a step forward and raised his fist. Instead of moving away, Ellen took a step forward, looking at him with cool defiance. In the same moment, Robert strode across the room.

"You bullying faker!" Robert cried. "Go! You'll have no money or even hospitality here. Go, and don't come back."

"I'll go," Patrick said, turning slowly away. "But I *will* be back. Count on that. You'll regret not paying me, and *she'll* regret insulting me. I'll settle the score with that one, too."

When the door was closed, Ellen said, "Robert, your refusal to pay him would have been sufficient to set him on this course. However, if my comments have increased his determination, I apologise."

Robert looked at her and shook his head. "He's like his brother. He's an angry man. He's a very bad man. Not at all the sort of man that you'd want as an enemy."

"What did he mean about something valuable, which your father might have stolen?"

"You don't miss anything, do you? Well, that is in my statement. If you wouldn't mind resuming your taking care of Mary, I shall go and add to it."

He looked down at his little sister. "Are you being brave, Mary?"

"I am managing, thank you."

He winced. "She hides in a protective layer of politeness. I don't like it. The poor girl. The sooner that this is over and out of the way, the better."

He turned away, hiding his emotion, and hurried up the stairs. We did our best to interest Mary in her toys.

We had soon done all that we could do with Mary's few toys. Before we began some games solely of imagination, using the stories which we knew, I said, "Ellen. We have been so engrossed in the terrible thing that happened that we haven't been thinking of Mary. Tomorrow, we must bring toys. Lots of toys, and books."

Ellen took a big breath and let it out. "Jo, you are right. I keep emphasising the importance of the small details, and I lose sight of the bigger things. It might apply to the investigation, too. I am like someone who is scrutinising footprints on a railway track, not noticing that a train is approaching."

I smiled. I liked it when she said honest things like that.

We were still doing our best to keep Mary occupied and distracted from the events of the day when her mother returned with Ellen's parents.

Mrs Stine gave us a thin smile and said, "Well, that's done. It's time to look to the future." After a brief hesitation, she asked in a general way, "How has it been here?"

"We did very well," Ellen said quickly. "Shall I make a cup of tea for you?"

"Oh. No. That's all right." Mrs Stine hurried after Ellen, who was already in the kitchen.

I understood why.

They soon came out together, with no tea. With an effort, Mrs Stine said, "Mr and Mrs Charteris. Would you like some tea, too?"

"No, thank you," Ellen's father replied. "Provided that you don't need us, we'll leave you in peace. But let us know if you need anything. Come on, girls."

"Yes," Ellen said, as though she had assessed her father's remarks, "it's probably best. We shall pop over tomorrow, Mrs Stine."

"Yes," Mrs Stine said distantly. "Thank you, all, for all you have done."

The poor woman now had to learn about the visit from her brother-in-law.

CHAPTER 6

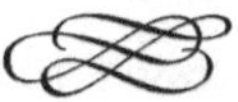

ARREST

After making a small pile of toys, dolls and books for Mary, I sat and thought. And after thinking, I decided. I put to one side some special old toys which had been passed down, or had a special meaning for me, and all the rest were for Mary. Why shouldn't the little girl who needed them have them? How could I justify keeping them when I no longer played with them?

"All those?" asked my mother when I struggled into the kitchen with a bulging sack.

"Yes," I replied. "I don't play with them, and Mary needs them."

"But don't you want to keep them for the future?"

"I don't need them now; why should I need them in the future?"

"Well, when you have children of your own."

"Mother! There is already a child who needs them."

"I'm not telling you not to give her a *few* things, but she isn't family. Not *our* family."

"She's a friend."

"Jo, she's the daughter of a servant of the parents of a girl whom you recently met at school. And anyway, I don't want you going down the street, hauling a bag of toys. Put some of them back."

In a moment, I saw the simple solution. Compromise. Take the toys a few at a time. "Yes, mother," I said. Mother smiled, not knowing that my brain had been stimulated by my new friend into seeing all aspects of a problem, including its solution.

My reduced load impressed Ellen, who had only a whip and top. With an embarrassed grimace, she said, "I didn't have the usual things as a child."

"I have plenty," I replied. "More to come on other visits."

She said no more until I was taking out the things for Mary. "Goodness, Jo. Is that how you passed your childhood, playing with those things? I'm not surprised that …."

"What? What doesn't surprise you?"

She shrugged and tried to look innocent. It didn't work. But I wasn't going to brood about it. Robert came down, and Mrs Stine passed round some scones which she had made. Mary was delighted with her toys, and it was a very pleasant gathering.

It didn't last.

A firm knock on the front door was followed almost immediately by the entrance of two policemen. One was clearly a detective, in a plain coat, a small man, with a compensating bristly moustache. The constable beside him was large, with a moustache which didn't bristle.

The detective looked around as though noting possible exits in case the three children and two adults decided to make a run for it.

"Robert Stine?" The detective looked sternly at Robert.

Robert looked left and right, then said, "Yes. Did you work that out, or was it a lucky guess?"

The response was excellent in quality, but deficient in tact.

"Don't try to be funny with me. I am Detective Mellor. I

am here to arrest you on suspicion of the murder of Leonard Stine."

Robert stood and walked towards the detective, but he repeated, quietly, to no-one in particular, "I didn't do it."

Ellen also stood and said, "Of course you didn't do it. Only an incompetent buffoon would think you had."

"And who are *you*?" the detective asked indignantly.

There was a voice outside the house. Detective Mellor turned and said, "Yes, thank you, Mr Stine. I've managed to work that out."

When he turned back, Ellen said, "I am Ellen Charteris. This is my associate, Jo Hopewell. We are investigating this case on behalf of the widow, and, of course, the person whom you have accused. Have you strong evidence for placing this man at the top of the long list of people who have been badly treated by the murdered man and should therefore be at least equally under suspicion?"

I had been watching the detective's face. I think that he was receiving Ellen's words very vaguely after the shock of the word 'investigating'. When he tried to reply, his voice sounded like a high note, plucked on a violin string. That wouldn't do. He scowled and used the time for the lowering of his voice to an appropriate growl.

"In all my years in the police force, I have never encountered such audacious insolence. At the very least, when I have finished my business here, my constable will escort you home and suggest to your father that a good hiding would be in order."

"In my few years of existence, I have frequently encountered such feeble displays of bluster when someone is quite out of his depth. If you prefer not to address your remarks to me, I suggest that you address them to the man whom you have accused of this crime. What is your evidence for arresting him?"

"Do *you* want to be arrested?"

"Nonsense," said Robert, roused into defending Ellen. "It is a reasonable question. I doubt that the answer will assist me, but we have the right to know."

"The *right to know*? No-one here has the right to know anything except the authorised officers of the law."

"Quite wrong," Ellen replied. "Even an accused man, his guilt not proved, has rights. He is not resisting arrest. He merely wishes to know the basis for his arrest."

The constable joined the discussion. "He didn't want to know anything until you poked your nose in, you young scamp."

Detective Mellor now gave the constable his look. "Yes, thank you, Constable." He turned and looked at Robert. "All right, then. Here it is. We have been informed that your mother complained to you about her treatment by her husband. She told us about that when she was interviewed. You were seen loitering by the canal, and you were seen to approach Leonard Stine and to argue fiercely with him. There was a struggle and you hit him. He was seen to fall into the canal, and you were seen to run off as someone approached, raising the alarm."

"One immediate question," Ellen began.

"You be quiet," the detective interrupted. "I don't want any further discussion of this. Young man, are you going to come peacefully to the police station with me?"

"Yes. That was always my intention."

"At least you'll be safe with the police," Ellen said. "They are incompetent, but you stand a much better chance of not being killed."

"BE … QUIET!" the detective bellowed.

"I hope," Ellen added quietly.

Detective Mellor knew that shouting at a girl wasn't in keeping with his carefully nurtured image of dour, stern, firmness. It was time to go.

"Right. Constable Harty, I'll escort the prisoner, and leave you to sort out all this other stuff and take these girls back to their homes."

"Yes, sir."

The detective said to the man outside, "As the brother of the deceased, and principal witness. you will be called to give evidence. What is your address?"

"47A, Causewayside. Above Mulliner's butcher shop."

"I know it. An officer will call on you in due course. He will ask you for a statement and you will be called as a witness in the trial."

"I understand."

"That will be all."

"Yes, sir."

Ellen's clear voice called, "And don't move to another address without informing the police."

The detective's head snapped round, first at Ellen, then at Constable Harty. "Do something about her," he growled.

"Yes, sir." Constable Harty watched the others leave, then said, "Right. Let's sort you lot out."

"And, Robert," Ellen called. "Don't forget to tell them about Patrick Stine's attempt to blackmail you."

There were various verbal explosions from the men outside. Ignoring them, Ellen said to me, "This is bad for Robert. We must work quickly to find the murderer."

Mary had watched and listened in silence, but now she shook her head, holding back the tears. Constable Harty thought he knew what to do. Constables have always suffered from the delusion that a large head, beneath a large helmet, and adorned with a thick moustache, suddenly thrust close to a child's face, is a comforting sight. Mary didn't think so. Her dam burst and out poured her tears.

"Perhaps it is for the best," Ellen said. "A good cry is probably what she needs."

"Yes, well," said the Constable. "The sooner you're both

back where you belong, the sooner I can return to more important work."

"I'd prefer to remain here for a while, but I expect you would refuse permission. Therefore, I suggest that my assistant and I return to our homes."

There was nothing to consider, being what Detective Mellor had ordered, but Constable Harty stood and considered before saying, "Yes. Well, that seems to be the most suitable way to proceed. Stay close to me. No tricks. No nonsense. And *no* talking!"

"That is a very desirable arrangement. It had been my intention to use the walk as an opportunity for thinking about this case, and my associate would never have maintained silence until we reached my home. Now, Jo, you must do as ordered by the constable."

I just about kept a straight face.

We said affectionate goodbyes to Mrs Stine and Mary and promised to return soon. The policeman was restless. Ellen said with a sigh, "Come on, then, Constable Harty. Number twenty four, the Crescent is our destination."

And off we went.

One large policeman and two girls.

I could feel his emanations of embarrassment. Each small group of restless children or loitering young men could not resist a smirk, and even a stifled snort of laughter, and there were some muffled comments, which Constable Harty ostentatiously pretended to ignore.

As we passed one group of sniggering young men, Ellen said, "Take no notice of them, Constable." He was clearly relieved when we arrived at Ellen's home. He was no longer the escort of two girls and he was about to be relieved of the presence of Ellen. But he couldn't restrain his admiration of The Crescent and Ellen's substantial house at the end of its substantial drive. "Very nice," he murmured.

When Mrs Charteris opened the door, she said, "Oh, my

goodness. What have you two been up to now? Please tell me you aren't in trouble."

Constable Harty politely waited for a few seconds, then cleared his throat. "Is this the Charteris residence?"

"Yes. I am Mrs Charteris. What is the problem?"

"Can you vouch for these young people?"

"Yes. Ellen is my daughter and Jo is her friend. Surely they have done nothing wrong."

"Well …." He have a little laugh, partly hidden by the large moustache. "I could say that they have been annoying a detective, but that would sound silly. Just, er, you girls mind how you go about whatever you're doing. We don't want someone's apple cart being upset."

Ellen said, "Thank you, Constable Harty. You have been very cooperative and tolerant. We shall do our best to stay out of Detective Mellor's way in future. As I'm sure you do."

He combined a cough and a growl, stroked his moustache and said, "Good. Right. I'll be off, then."

CHAPTER 7

THE STATEMENT

Mother was in deep discussion with the butcher boy when I called, "Just popping out with Ellen."

"What? Oh. Right," was her distracted response.

"That worked well," I said as we walked briskly to the Stines' house.

"Yes, but you shouldn't have to be furtive or apologetic about joining me in my investigation. They should be pleased that you are doing this."

"Mother wants me to be normal. To be fair to her, that is what I had always been until you appeared. Very normal."

"Define 'normal'."

"I suppose it means behaving in accordance with social and parental standards."

"Would that help Mrs Stine, Mary and Robert?"

"Well, the police ..." She stopped and made me stop, too. She looked at me severely and said, "Go on, Jo. The police have arrested Robert because of what his malevolent uncle said. Now, tell me how confident you are about the police."

I let out a big sigh. "Not at all."

"And being normal?"

"Counts for nothing," I answered with a laugh. "Come on. Let's go and investigate."

"We're already making progress," she said as we hurried on. "Your brain is fully functional again, mine always is, and the first step is to read Robert's statement. I hope that it isn't too well hidden."

It wasn't. Mrs Stine was ready for us, and ready with the statement. Now that the funeral was out of the way, she had become practical and determined.

"I know all, or most of this, because Robert told me, but I'll let you read it because it will be clearer than if I chattered away. I'll keep Mary occupied while you read it, although she has plenty to occupy her, with all the things that you kindly brought."

We sat together on the settee, shoulder to shoulder, in order to read the document simultaneously. But I asked Ellen to take her time. I didn't want her to be finishing a page while I was half way down it.

"Don't worry," she said. "I'll be reading and thinking."

And so, we read and thought.

Statement by Robert Stine.

My regiment is the Fourteenth Foot of the Royal Blues, currently engaged in the interminable war in Kurukhstan. Although our argument is with the rebels who were ruining their country, the rights and wrongs of that do not concern those who are loyal to their Country and their command. We do as we are told, and when we lack orders in a crisis, we do as we expect to have been told. It is a tough life, in which tough friendships and occasional tough enmities are formed.

Before and during battle, our soldiers are as disciplined as any. However, after battle, there is sometimes a relaxing of discipline. Mostly, this involves some careless frivolity, even drunkenness, and those in charge must be at their strongest to maintain order. On no account, at any level, is any aggressive, or even disrespectful, behaviour permitted towards those who are not involved in the fighting, or those who have been defeated in fighting. Sometimes, in a variety of ways, regrettable things are done.

After the taking of Kalahar, there were indications of laxity, and our Colonel was forced to take drastic action. Severe punishments were imposed, both to maintain discipline and to demonstrate to the Kurukhstan people that we were an honourable enemy. In support of this, we were forbidden access to the local temple, where as always, the poor people who worshipped respected the inviolacy of religious artefacts which would be worth a fortune back home.

Although merely a corporal, I took very seriously both the orders and the reasons for them. Even within the necessary constraints, there were still many temptations, and I needed to be very strong. I was relieved when we received our orders to move on to the next place of dispute. I wasn't keen to be involved in another battle, but I wanted to be away.

One of my fellows, another corporal, was one of those people who come and go, without saying where they are going or where they have been. He wasn't a bad lad, and we were sort of friends.

We were soon in action, at a place called Taliwar. A typical mountain battle, with much aimless, in the true sense, firing, and occasional skirmishes. One of these caught us thoroughly off-guard because we believed that our bit of the line was on a steep ridge that couldn't be climbed. Well, the enemy managed it, suddenly appearing a few yards in front of us, with guns, swords and spears. We managed to repel them, but my corporal friend, fighting next to me, was killed, shot in the chest.

In trying to locate the wound, and perhaps stop the flow

of blood, I found something which filled me with horror. A large diamond. I had no doubt that he had sneaked into the temple and stolen it. And I had no doubt that it would be of great importance to the people of Kalahar. I didn't even think of its financial value. I thought only of the importance of returning it.

Well, that would have to wait. Before that, there was the important matter of staying alive and repulsing the enemy. This wasn't one of those battles that are decided by an irresistible onslaught. This was the sort of battle that mountain folk relish. Hours would pass without a shot, someone would adjust his position or reach for a drink, and down he would go with a bullet through his head. It was a battle in which unwavering concentration was needed. There was no going forward and no going back. We all stayed at our posts amongst the rocks, looking for opportunities to shoot, while avoiding being shot.

But even the mountain soldiers like to vary their tactics, or perhaps even they become bored with waiting. Again, forward they crept, and suddenly appeared, yelling and firing, unnerving and confusing us. But we kept our discipline, keeping our bodies still while we concentrated on firing accurately and effectively. But my luck was out that day. One of the enemy, shot in the stomach, staggered about, still firing. One bullet went into my left arm, one into my left shoulder, another into my right thigh, each one doing a lot of damage. But those were the only wounds, so I suppose it would be more accurate to say that my luck was *in*.

In the usual daft way, I was all for trying to keep going, but the sergeant said he wasn't going to have someone who couldn't fight effectively consuming rations. During a lull, I was removed for treatment by the local sawbones, which was very unpleasant, then sent to a makeshift hospital, and then I began the long journey back to this Country. It was such a long journey that I suggested my body had done all the healing it was going to do, and that I should be sent back. But we were in the middle of a military procedure, in the middle of a war, and no-one was going to risk his career by disobeying an order which required me to have a couple of weeks of convalescence, a short home visit, then my return to the far away fray.

And that is what happened, and that is the end of the dull part about my being wounded and coming home.

All this time, I managed to keep hold of the diamond, constantly moving it from one bit of clothing to another or to my kit bag, depending on what was being done to me at any time. I didn't want anyone to know about the diamond because it was large and clearly very valuable. I didn't trust anyone, not friend, criminal or government. That diamond was going to be returned to its rightful place.

So, one wrongly removed diamond with one wounded soldier, determined to return it as soon as he was declared fit again.

Now, as you would expect, a temporary hospital a little way behind the lines, in the midst of a hectic series of battles, is bound to be a busy place, with wounded soldiers, medical staff and those official people who try to maintain some sort of order. What you wouldn't expect is to see one of the locals, dressed in his local garments, appearing to have no function at all, hovering, and watching. And what he seemed to be watching mostly was *me*. This went on for the couple of days that I was in the hospital. It wasn't constant, but I had the impression that when he looked, it was for the purpose of confirming that I was still there.

Clearly, what he didn't expect was that a soldier with a few bullet wounds would be sent thousands of miles to recover in his own country. As I limped out to join the other invalids in the wagon, I saw him, looking disgusted and perplexed. In spite of the seriousness, I chuckled to see his consternation. Far from having the simple task of waylaying me as I returned to the battle, he now had the prospect of following me over the vast distance between his country and mine.

Of course, I thought many times of trying to establish a form of communication between us, with the intention of ascertaining that he was a proper custodian of the diamond. But what if he weren't? What if he wanted possession of the diamond for a dishonest purpose? Perhaps if I had stayed longer in that hospital I could have had a discussion with him. But suddenly, with unusual consideration, the Army was sending me home to recover and recuperate, and my thoughts were already turning to that happy prospect.

It was a long journey home, enlivened by the scenery and by the comradeship of similarly, or worse, injured soldiers. But it is no denigration of the scenery or the company to say that I was very pleased to be on the boat which brought me over the last leg of my journey.

It was on this last stage that I was alarmed to see my observer again. He was now wearing a suit in place of his national clothing, but I recognised him. As before, he was *watching*, showing no inclination to approach me. I began to suspect that he was waiting for the right moment in which to remove the diamond from me and take it back to his country without any disturbance and pursuit. From that time, I began to dread being alone, and I was always in company or on the alert. My bedroom door was always locked, and my service revolver always ready. Even my three days of convalescence up North consisted largely of my doing my own watching, and even listening.

After three days, I insisted that I was recovered and needed only a quick visit home before returning to my duties as a soldier. More than anything, even the prospect of some time with my mother and sister, I wanted to be rid of the diamond, which felt like a great weight.

There isn't much more to tell. I came home, leaving my bag in the front room. It is my belief that my father entered quietly, saw my bag and immediately had a rummage for anything of value, and found, and took, the diamond. Then, he slammed the door, pretending to have arrived that moment, scrounged some money and left. When I heard all that he'd been doing, then realised that the diamond had disappeared, I followed him and berated him. He attacked me, and I pushed him away. He fell into the canal. I was helping him out when there were footsteps, and he shouted that he was being murdered. In that moment, to my great regret, and shame, I panicked and ran.

Sometime after that, he was killed, and, it must be assumed, the diamond was taken. His brother came and tried to blackmail me, offering to say nothing about the supposed murder by me. I refused, and I expect him to concoct a story, which the police will believe.

This is the end of my statement. If anyone can shine a light on the darkness of this mystery, I shall be very much obliged.

"He means me," Ellen said, "and I shall."

CHAPTER 8

PATRICK STINE IS ANGRY AND DANGEROUS

It was clear even to us that we couldn't justify continuing daily visits to Mrs Stine and Mary on the grounds that they needed us. Besides, Mrs Stine was back helping Ellen's parents, with Mary in close attendance. But at least that made it easier to carry out our little subterfuges, such as picnics and visits to the art gallery, the library and the museum. After the involvement in the dark events concerning Mrs Stine, such excursions were welcomed.

Of course, we did briefly do all those things, to avoid indulging in deceit. Indeed, there were times when I was reluctant to resume our investigation. But for the sake of this narrative, I shall omit the brief honesty visits and concentrate on the important events. I shall also exclude, other than this brief summarising mention, my Mother's constant attempts to complicate everything that Ellen and I planned to do.

"A picnic? Well, of course I'm not going to let you go off without an adequate supply of food and drink."

She even pulled a small hamper from beneath the stairs. "If you'd told me before, I'd have baked a cake. I think there's some left in the pantry."

I didn't want to tell lies, but I could hardly tell her that we were going to be busy with a murder investigation. "It isn't *just* a picnic. We're going exploring."

"Not caves or potholes! Not deep rivers or reservoirs! Not places where bad people go! Not that canal again."

I tried again, trying to combine plausibility with reality, and without actually being dishonest. "No. Nothing like that. You know how historical tours are arranged, to look at medieval parts of the city, the stocks and the old gaol, and the site of the Saxon court; well, we're going to be going round the City, looking for interesting things. We'll be quite safe. But we'll be doing a lot of walking and don't want to have a lot to carry."

"If you're doing a lot of walking, you'll need more food."

"I shall have a big appetite for my tea."

With some residual reluctance, she settled for that and made a couple of sandwiches, which she carefully wrapped. She gave me some coppers with which to buy some ginger beer, and I was all set.

"I want you back by three," she said.

That was understandable, though not desirable. The problem, as Ellen put it, was that when you have a finishing time, you plan backwards from it. But she understood the parental concern, too. Her parents had not been so specific, but had settled for vague bits of advice about being careful with things and cautious with people.

"There is some irony," Ellen said as we walked along busy streets "that throughout our murder investigation, our biggest danger will be carts and carriages and their horses."

I agreed with her. Moments later, we had entered Cooper Street, where they were having what I believe is formally termed vehicular congestion. Hundreds of them, all sorts and sizes, seemed to be playing a vast game of solitaire, trying constantly to move into a space as soon as the present occupier managed to move to another space. Eventual direction seemed to play no part; it was a constant shuffle into inadequate spaces. There was much shouting, mostly of the general sort, but some it specifically directed at a particular driver, often accompanied by, or responded by, an invitation to dismount and engage in physical combat.

"There ain't room to have a fight," one potential combatant protested, his anger dissolving into laughter.

"You're right there," was the reply, and, having released a little pressure, both settled down to wait more or less patiently for some progress to be made.

Ellen said, "It's the horses that suffer most, being kicked and whipped to go forward quickly a few feet, then jerked back and told to stand still, then sent forward again. So most things continue to go, even in this frantically terminating century. The policeman walking the street knows that there are people whom heredity and social circumstance have combined to make vicious and callous. And because of that, he believes that there must always be people who will steal and murder. He considers it to be an inevitable condition of the human being. But it is not. All people are *more likely* to do certain things, but they can resist, they can change. Some people become the opposite of what they used to be."

"That's interesting," I said. "But what has it to do with horses?"

"Well, because horses are strong, have four legs and broad backs, and are generally docile, there is an assumption that their reason for existing is to pull loads for humans and to carry humans on their backs."

"And sometimes to race for humans."

"Yes. That, too. But I maintain that horses were put on Earth to be horses. Nothing to do with us. If we could ask a horse to pull something, and the horse could understand and agree willingly to do it, that would be another matter. But there is no means of understanding, no means of discussing. Therefore, horses should be allowed to go their way, and we should go ours."

I couldn't help thinking that here was another reason for the probability that Ellen Charteris was going to annoy people for the rest of her life. Teachers, policemen, and, well, all sorts of people who believe that the purpose of horses is to perform tasks for humans. Even I could see the potential dangers in that sort of thinking. It could lead to all sorts of things. But what would bother people the most was her detached, logical thinking. She wasn't satisfied with the belief that something must be right because it's what we've always done. Horses pulled carts, and women weren't detectives. In both cases, she demanded the reason, based on reasoning.

Back to the investigation, Ellen wanted to begin by going down to the canal again. On the way, we both looked carefully for any signs of … anything. I thought that I was looking closely, but Ellen made my efforts seem casual. She frequently darted, stooped and peered, reminding me of a wading bird which I once saw on holiday, in pursuit of small fish and mollusks hiding in the sand and rocks.

When we reached the broad area where the murder occurred, she moved very slowly, and I could almost feel the intensity of her scrutiny. Several times during the search, she seemed to find things, but she didn't say anything to me. So far as this went, I think that I had ceased to have any relevance for her, and might as well have been a small tree or a hitching post. If she had been anyone else, I might have been nervous as she leaned over the edge, crouched, and once turned almost upside down as she looked at something that was out of my sight, close to the water.

She announced the termination of that part of the investigation by straightening her back and saying, "Hmm." Then she looked at the public house in which Leonard Stine had had his last drink.

I read her thoughts. "Ellen! That is not only a public house; it is one which forbids women, especially one as young as you. They will not permit you to enter, and even if they did, it would not be safe."

"On the other hand, such places as this have no objection to serving women and children at the back door, filling their jugs with beer."

"That's because the women and children have been sent to buy beer for the men at home."

"Do they know that? Do they care? Do they object to the presence of women and children merely because it would interfere with their manly pleasure of being loud, vulgar and generally obnoxious?"

"We're digressing," I grumbled.

"Indeed we are, but only because you raised an unnecessary objection."

"Then you do not intend to go into the Spread Eagle?"

"That is correct. Now, let us go to the Spread Eagle in order that I may ask some questions."

She walked briskly away and I didn't bother to object. After a few steps, I understood. At this time of the morning, the door of the public house was open and the landlord and another man were rolling in a barrel of beer and another man was sweeping the contents of the floor out into the street, where, like their inebriated customers, they entered the public domain and were no longer a concern of theirs.

Ellen stopped at the threshold. The man who was sweeping out grunted, "Shift yourself, unless you want to be swept out, too."

Ellen seemed neither to see nor hear him. She stood and looked into the dim room, in which a few men were already drinking. Ellen called, "Your attention, please! Does anyone know anything about the recent murder of Leonard Stine?"

The drinking men ignored her. The man with the brush snorted. The landlord snarled, "Clear off."

"Ah," Ellen said, sounding pleased and rubbing her hands as she turned to me. "You see, we *are* making progress. These people have clearly indicated that they have something to hide. Probably several things. I shall report this to Detective Mellor."

"What are you to Detective Mellor?" the landlord asked, reluctantly giving way to his curiosity.

Ellen walked into the room. I nervously followed her. The landlord looked shocked and embarrassed, especially after exchanging a glance with his clearly indignant customers. "Here," he began, but Ellen flicked the word away.

"Relax, all of you. You have daughters, wives and mothers. I am one of the same species and I am visiting very briefly. Nothing to be afraid of or upset about. Go on with your drinking and conversations. Now, landlord, I am what you might call the unofficial branch of Detective Mellor's department," Ellen said. "I do things which, for various reasons, a formally-appointed police officer would not do. I have a strong preference for directness and forthrightness, and a low opinion of ingratiating diplomacy. I do not wish to placate you, mollify you or be accepted into your good books. I want only facts. And the only facts in which I am interested are those which might be of use in finding the murderer of Leonard Stine."

"I told the police. Leonard Stine was a nasty piece of work who came here with enough money to make him a bit more nasty, and when he'd run out of money, he drank someone else's beer, then staggered out into the night. And that's the last that we saw of him alive. One of our people left early. He saw a struggle, blows from a weapon and the victim fall into the canal. He rushed back in and told us and most of us rushed out to see, perhaps assist, bad as he was, but Leonard Stine was beyond assistance. Someone went off and told a policeman, and that was it, and there you are, missy, and we'll be much obliged to see you leave now. Or, to put it another way, clear off."

Ellen raised a finger. "And the name of the person who saw a struggle?"

"None of your business."

"Ah. Patrick Stine said that it was he, so in the absence of other information, I shall believe him."

"Then why did you ask?"

"Believing Pastrick Stine does not come easily to me."

"Well, that's your problem. Clear off."

"Very willingly. I have what I wanted. I have no desire to remain longer than necessary. Thank you for your patience and assistance."

"Oh, you're very welcome." The tone and the grin of blatant sarcasm.

"Excellent," Ellen said, turning away. I was happy to follow her, but I tried to conceal my eagerness to be well away from those horrible and dangerous men. As we walked beside the canal, I looked back a few times, expecting to be followed, knocked on the head and flung into the water.

As we went up the steps and I began to feel safe, at least for a while, I asked, "Where next?"

"I think that we shall visit the neighbourhood of Mr Patrick Stine."

"I thought that having started at the bottom, we'd be going up. You're suggesting that we start at the bottom and go down."

"The area has its Patrick Stines, but it has a lot of good people, too. Most of them are just poor. Poverty does not encourage the finer feelings, but Causewayside has its workshops and its chapel, and people still go to it."

"How do you know so much about it?"

"I asked my father to take me to some of these places. I wanted to speak, and think, with the benefit of at least some superficial knowledge."

Not for the first time, I wondered whether this was really a girl of fourteen. I asked, "Were you ever a child, in the usual way? Did you ever scrape your knee and cry? Did you ever have a doll? Were you ever afraid of the dark?"

"I did graze my knee once. I immediately saw no benefit to be gained by crying. I diverted my attention to a study of the circumstances, and my own carelessness, which led to the fall, and the pain soon stopped. I was given a doll, probably as a test, when I was four. I did not see the point of it: a china representation of something which grotesquely combined the features of a baby and a young lady, and which I knew was not real. When I was very young, I had a nightmare, almost strangled myself and suffocated in the bedclothes, and called for help. My mother refused to turn on the light. She talked to me in the dark, drawing my attention to the brightly gleaming stars. She said that turning on the light would make me think that the dark was a bad and fearsome thing, to be cast away by the simultaneous appearance of my mother and the light."

"Have you never been silly or naughty?"

"I have never been intentionally silly. As to naughty, some might say that I have been extremely naughty in the way in which I have spoken to various adults during the last few days. Some of it was necessary, some of it was strategic, and some of it was mischievous. I have deceived my parents and encouraged you to deceive yours. I am probably the naughtiest child that you know. However, my naughtiness always has a good purpose."

I was still savouring her eloquence when we entered a narrow passage, and from that we entered Causewayside. On the far side, it was a strange mixture of small, and tall, terraced houses,

many converted into apartments, shops and workshops, including a boat-builder and two blacksmiths. On the side on which we stood, it seemed to be just tall terraced houses.

Knowing that we had walked in a straight line from the canal, I commented that Causewayside ran parallel to it.

"That's right," she agreed. "This city is an odd combination of straight lines and tangled knots."

Peering across the way, she said, "The display of numbers is erratic and confusing, but there is Mr Mulliner's butcher's shop, above which Mr Patrick Stine lives, and probably that door to the side of the entrance is for the use of the lodger. Well, this is convenient. It is perfectly reasonable for people to stand outside a butcher's shop and look, then go inside."

However, we had barely begun our pretence of being discerning customers, when Mr Mulliner hurried out of the shop. Apart from his height, everything about him was large. Even his ears would have caused some excited movement on the scales. He looked at us with those eyes that sparkle not with merriment but with animosity.

"Are you intending to buy?" he asked sharply.

Ellen replied without looking at him. "We are looking at what you have. My parents were very specific as to quality. However, if our scrutiny bothers you, we could go somewhere else."

"No, oh, no. No problem at all. It's just that a lot of young people hang around, often pinching stuff when my back's turned. Not you, of course. And, then, I haven't seen you round here before."

"My father is very particular. One might say fussy. We have lived in King Street for three years, but he has yet to find a satisfactory butcher. I have made it my duty to explore on his behalf."

"Very commendable."

"Clearly, you know most of your customers. Is your trade mainly local?"

"We do a lot of local trade, mainly for offal, chitterlings, trotters, tails, bits and pieces. But I have a lot of customers who come from all over, some of them in carriages."

"It certainly seems to be good quality. Have you a printed sheet of what you provide? For my father."

"I certainly do. But do tell your father that what I have varies because I insist on the best quality. I'd rather be short of something that sell inferior produce."

"He'll appreciate that."

"Wait here and I'll fetch one."

"That's all right. I'll come in and save you the trouble."

I stayed outside, trying to avoid any suggestion of intrusion. I stepped back to have a better view of the place. A window above me opened and a voice called, "Look out below," followed by a laugh and the arrival of a bowlful of water, just to the side of me. It missed me, but splashed over my legs. There was another laugh, and I looked up to show that I didn't share the amusement.

Neither, as soon as he saw me, did Patrick Stine. He drew in his head quickly, and I heard heavy footsteps in his room. I rushed to the door of the shop. Ellen was still chatting to the affable butcher.

"Ellen, we must go now," I called, trying to express urgency without making Mr Mulliner suspicious. Ellen glanced at me. She knew that there must be danger for me to take charge. I looked up to show the source of the danger. At the same time, we heard the heavy footsteps on the wooden stairs.

I saw Ellen nod her understanding, then stubbornly turn and await the imminent arrival of the angry man. With more heavy footsteps, he appeared at the front of the shop.

Ellen faced him coolly. "How extraordinary," she said. "You keep appearing."

"Yes," he replied, not exactly agreeing. "First I found you at my brother's house. Now I find you at *my* house."

"This man's excellent shop, actually. I am hoping that my father will place regular orders with Mr Mulliner."

The butcher looked at Ellen, but spoke to Stine. "What's this about?"

Stine shook his head. "I told you about a snooping girl. Well, when she comes right into your shop, no doubt asking a lot of questions, and you don't even put two and two together; I mean, this isn't a difficult one to work out."

Ellen guessed that the butcher wasn't pleased by the disparaging remarks. She winked and screwed up her nose. "Tell him what we have been discussing, Mr Mulliner."

"Well, meat. And orders for meat. That's all."

"Just meat, Mr Stine," added Ellen. "Nothing at all about you."

"You heard me give my address to that copper. Bit of a coincidence that you come here shortly after."

"Don't you think that it *might* be a coincidence, and that I came here because I had heard that Mr Mulliner is an excellent butcher?"

"No."

"Ah. You don't think he's an excellent butcher."

"Don't you try to twist my words. You're here because you're spying on me."

"Because you tried to blackmail your nephew? The less that I see of you, the better. Now, I do have other matters to attend to, and wish to conclude my business with Mr Mulliner. Are you on your way out?"

He thrust his fist into Ellen's face. She feigned alarm. "Oh, Mr Stine. Fearsome."

He snarled and growled in one rough sound. "You keep out of my way. That's all," and went back through the shop. Ellen looked at the confused butcher. "May we resume?" she said, almost sweetly.

"Are you sure it's my meat that you're interested in, and not my lodger?"

"Mr Mulliner, I promise you that as soon as I arrive home, I shall willingly present your sheet to my father, with my comments on what I have seen presented for sale. I do not make his decisions for him, and must be circumspect about offering an opinion, but I shall report honestly on what I have seen and heard, omitting your uncouth lodger. I can't reasonably do any more."

"No. Of course. I understand."

So did I. Ellen was very skilful at not telling a lie while thoroughly misleading people. I noticed, too, that since she was no longer required to play the part of schoolgirl, her confident demeanour had strengthened. She seemed to become more detached and bold with each obstacle.

As we walked away along Causewayside, she folded the sheet of paper and said, “I shall, of course, present it to my father, with some simple comments about what we saw on display. Mr Mulliner is not the best of people, but he seemed to be ignorant of what his lodger has been doing. I'll give him the benefit of the doubt. And I shall do as I said.”

“We’ve confirmed that Stine is living there. Did you find out anything else?”

“It is a fine day. Though not by any means a follower of the fashions, Mr Stine was clearly dressed for going out. But when I asked him whether he was going out, I saw a flicker of worry in his eyes before he responded in his customary manner, and he quickly returned to his room. I also saw that there is a back door, leading to a yard.”

“Is all that connected, and intended to make things clear?”

“Of course. This doorway will do very well. I’d prefer to have the better view from across the road, but he might be watching.”

“We’re going to watch him leave?”

“Provided that I have surmised correctly and he does so, yes.”

“Then what? Oh, no. No, Ellen.”

“I shan’t be up there for long. And you’ll keep watch for me.”

“What am I supposed to do if he comes back? Cough very loudly?”

“Just go, quickly.”

“And leave you?”

“One in danger is better than two. Ah. There he goes. Glancing round and walking quickly away.”

"Ellen! Why don't I follow him? That might be useful, and when he returns, I could run on ahead and warn you."

"Well done, Jo. I didn't want to ask. Stay well back. He might expect to be followed. Be cautious. And be careful. Off you go, then, before you lose him."

Of course she had already thought of it. But I didn't know that when I thought of it. And to have the same thought was a big improvement. And now here I was, suddenly promoted to active and independent duty. I preferred that to waiting nervously on guard.

Stop that, I chided myself. Stop congratulating yourself and concentrate. This job must be done well or not at all.

The problem with staying well back was that he had gone down St Nicholas Street and was now amongst the stalls, shops and winding lanes of the market area, where it would be very easy to lose him in a moment. He made it more difficult by constantly turning this way and that, and soon I began to suspect that he was doing it on purpose.

Suddenly, he hurried out of the market area,and crossed Wine Street to Castle Green, dodging between the horses and carriages. I hesitated, then carefully followed. There weren't many people about. The rather rough paths deterred the pushers of perambulators, and there was no pond or bandstand. Just St Peter's Church and the ruins of the Norman castle amongst the trees and bushes, and they didn't combine to encourage liveliness.

And some lively people was what I wanted as I followed Stine through the shade of the trees. I wanted some families with children, retired military gentlemen, perhaps a strolling policeman. I wanted some city bustle. This quiet area, with the city sounds already muffled, was not the sort of area in which I wanted to be alone with Patrick Stine. Nervousness was steadily growing into fear, which sharpened when I could no longer see him.

Was I still going towards him, or was he coming towards me?

I wanted to turn and run, back to the crowded, busy streets, but I didn't want him to see me and become suspicious, and then go back before Ellen was safely out of the way.

I had been trusted with this job.

If only I could at least hear him. Had he merely gone ahead, or turned, or decided to stop and rest? Was he waiting for someone? Perhaps me? If he were still, then my movements would be heard.

Admit it, I told myself: you are no good for this sort of work.

I walked slowly on, wincing with each rustle and twig snap.

The ground rose a little, then dropped again. As I went over this little hill, I saw that he had stopped and was facing me. Just standing there, waiting for me. This wasn't the location for trying bluff or for any form of pretence. I turned back. Very close to me, standing on the brow of the little hill was Torrance Kiddle. He used to stand outside the school gates and shout nasty things. Too stupid even for factory work, malnourished by tobacco and idleness, he had an old, grey face and a twisted, knobbly body. After leaving school, he had become a large lout. Soon, he would be a larger lout.

He had a fondness for grinning at the suffering of others.

It was clear that I was trapped.

Oddly, I thought at least it meant that Ellen was safe.

"Where's the other one?" Stine called irritably over my shoulder.

"It was only this one that followed you. You just said you were going to be followed and I was to follow whoever followed you. Which I did."

After my first thought, about Ellen, my next thought was the obvious one: I needed to run as quickly as I could. Two louts against my general lightness and fitness. I could do it. And I'd do some hefty shouting on the way.

Go!

It is important not to hesitate or reveal your intentions and I sprinted … for one step. I should have glanced down first. My foot went into one of those holes that mysterious creatures like to dig. It wasn't a deep hole but deep enough to make me lurch and topple. I went down with a thud and slid on the grass. Two pairs of hands immediately gripped me. I was dragged to my feet and shoved against a tree.

"Where's the other one?" Stine's words and spittle stung my face.

"My friend? She's gone home. I was just trying to be helpful."

"By following me?"

"Ellen's investigation requires the gathering of information on various people. You happen to be involved. That does''t mean we suspect you of a crime. It's just information-gathering."

I thought it was a plausible explanation that no reasonable person could resent. Of course, Patrick Stine was not a reasonable person. He snarled, "I don't like to be followed and snooped on. I don't like to be suspected. I don't like to be interfered with, especially by a couple of precocious brats."

I was determined not to crumple under the physical and mental pressure. "I assure you that no offence was intended. We just want your brother's killer to be brought to justice."

"*Then why are you following me*?" he roared, the hot stickiness of his breath even worse than the noise.

"Keep it down, Pat," his associate muttered.

"Just information-gathering," I replied.

He had just started to do a contemptuous repeat of my reply when the thought which I didn't want to occur to him, occurred to him. He seemed to look right through me, and right through the tree behind me. "She's at my place, isn't she?" he said Ignoring my denials, he shook his head and murmured, "Of *course*, she is. *In* there. Not just watching from outside. And you were going to run on ahead and warn her when I returned. Well, you won't be doing that. Grab an arm, Torrance. We'll put her in the ruin."

Patrick Stine was one of those people who are always angry, the only variation being increased anger. He displayed a smile of anger. He looked as though he were gnawing a bone. He pulled from his pocket some leather strands. "These will keep you out of mischief while I go back and catch your friend, and take her straight to the police station. We'll come back for you later, when it's dark."

After a quick check that no-one was around, they pulled me, almost carried me, up the hill to the Castle ruin.

Apart from some bits of outer wall, most of the ruin consisted of heaps of fallen stones, through which plants were growing. The two men scrambled over several of these heaps, dragging me, ignoring my cries as the stones scraped my knees.

"This'll do," said Stine, jumping down a high pile of stones and pulling me after him.

Torrance lost his balance and fell awkwardly, which pleased me.

"I'm always prepared," Stine said, taking out some pieces of cord. "Hold out your hands, wrists together. He tied the strands very tight, then tipped me over and bound my ankles, also very tight.

"Right. Let's go and settle the other meddler."

As he prepared to follow his master, Torrance grinned. His effort was worse than Stine's, merely conveying the full force of his idiocy. I laughed at him and shook my head. The grin became a scowl. It was no improvement.

As soon as they had left, I began to wriggle about, trying to find a sharp bit of stone. "Come *on*," I cried impatiently. "One of you must have a sharp edge. I must warn Ellen."

"That won't be necessary", said that familiar voice.

I spun round and cried, "Ellen!"

She was already opening her penknife and with brisk strokes, she cut through all the strands.

"As you set off after him, I saw him click his fingers, and that accomplice of his followed you. I decided that you were a higher priority than my examination of the room. My apology for not intervening sooner, but provided that you were not being harmed, I preferred to let them rise into their smug ignorance."

"What if Stine had decided that the simplest way of dealing with me was to cut my throat?"

"I'd have made sure that he was brought to justice."

"Oh. Thank you. I feel much better now."

Did she even hear me? Probably just as background noise, like the occasional barking of a dog or the clatter of a coach's wheels. She was thinking. Here and now were already in the past, and her thoughts were already sprinting into the future.

"That will be best," she decided. "Come on. Let's follow them."

We soon caught up with them, and I felt some pleasure in turning the tables, or putting the

table back where it was. Anyway, they thought that I was securely tied up in the castle ruin and that they were going to catch Ellen in Stine's room; and instead, we were carefully following them.

"We don't even have to be particularly careful about it, "Ellen said. "They certainly aren't expecting to be followed."

But we were very cautious as we approached Causewayside, knowing that they would be, too. "Huh," Ellen said. "Stine suspects that subtlety is the thing here, but he has no idea of how to do it. In a few moments, he will go for the fast and direct approach."

He did. Leaving Torrance to watch the front, he dashed across the road and round the back of the shop. We saw him appear at the window, looking annoyed. Ellen suggested that we now stroll into Causewayside. "Without a care in the world, and without a glance towards either of them," she added.

"I *know* that they are looking," I whispered. "I can feel it."

"Yes," Ellen agreed. "But he will now plan his next move, and we must plan ours. Ours is more complicated because we are still trying to find the killer of the other Mr Stine, and for all that we know, *this* Mr Stine might be no more than an irritating distraction."

"I doubt that."

"So do I."

CHAPTER 9

A SHORT FAMILY INTERLUDE

I had known that our annual week at the seaside was approaching, but I hadn't known about the proposed preceding few days at an elderly cousin of my father.

"It was a late decision, following an out-of-the-blue invitation," Father explained. "It's Great Aunt Nancy's eightieth birthday."

The rest of the explanation followed, but it wasn't necessary. This branch of the family called gatherings at the drop of a hat. Birthdays, anniversaries, engagements and weddings, funerals; the summons went out, like the blowing of a tribal horn, and the hordes made their way from all points of the compass to the Elms, where cousin Alistair and his wife Marjory hosted and hostessed as though it were their great vocation.

At least the seaside had some minor distractions to compensate for my absence from Ellen and the investigation. Everywhere that I went in the large house and large garden of the Elms, I was expected to play my role of little girl, and to suffer the two horrors of constant hugging and constant interrogation about what I was learning at school.

This treatment was more vexing than usual because of my association with Ellen. I certainly didn't feel like a little girl, even for the purpose of pleasing the distant relations who derived such pleasure from me. I longed to answer their polite questions with "Oh, I'm currently investigating a brutal murder. One of the people involved captured me, tied me up and left me in a ruined castle."

"Yes, dear," the person would say. "That sounds jolly exciting. But I think that you ought to imagine more suitable things. Girls don't have adventures."

Eventually, after a few hours of being fussed over, I did lose my patience and responded to an intense patting of my head by purring. My mother descended on me with the speed that we all want to see in our constables. I was taken out to look at the flowers and severely reprimanded.

"Why can't you be like your cousins?" Mother asked.

Perhaps the greatest of many annoyances in the life of a child is the frequent comparison with most of the other children in the family, the school or the neighbourhood. I almost protested, but there was too much to be said, causing the verbal equivalent of that recent traffic congestion. I settled for a sigh.

"And it's no good sighing," Mother said. "You ought to be pleased to be with so many members of your family, especially your charming and well-behaved cousins."

That made me feel worse.

I wanted to tell her that I, yes, *I*, was an Assistant Very Private Detective, currently playing an important role in the investigation of a murder. Wasn't that much more important than being charming and well-behaved?

No, she would probably say.

I sighed for my benefit. I had outgrown my family and school and everything that I was supposed to be, and I could never return to what I had been.

Ellen had changed everything.

When the great family gathering had been left behind, like a museum of antipathies, and we had chugged on a lumbering train to Selsby Cove, I cheered up, determined that if I couldn't investigate the murder with Ellen, at least I could practise observation and curiosity by investigating the rock pools and cliffs. My parents didn't exactly let me go off on my own, and they didn't neglect or ignore me, but I was allowed a little time to myself. We all went down to the beach together and they would spend most of the day preparing to do things and organising what they intended to do. The rocks weren't far away, and when my parents occasionally came out of their preparations and checked on me, I was always in sight or close enough to respond to the first anxious call.

We had left behind the city of carts, cabs and coaches, footpads and sooty air, but my mother persisted in seeing constant danger in the gently lapping sea.

Sitting on the rocks, watching the waves, peering into the dark depths of small pools, was comforting, reminding me that no matter how many terrible crimes people committed, the sea kept coming and going with its infinite patience. And in each rock pool, there were thousands of things, living and never having lived, some of them many times as old as any people.

And in each rock pool, there were thousands of mysteries.

Botanists, biologists, archaeologists, all studied and worked to unravel the mysteries.

Well, that's what Ellen and I were doing, and were going to do. Wherever, and however we found them.

The world would be our rock pool.

All that made me feel better about things.

With my searching in the pools, a trip round the bay and some long walks along the cliff top, and plenty of food at the guest house, the week passed pleasantly, and I returned refreshed and eager to resume with Ellen. After the inevitable delays for helping with the unpacking and washing of clothes, then my school essay about my holiday, which Mother insisted that I write while it was so fresh in my memory, I hurried round to Ellen's house.

CHAPTER 10

BACK TO WORK, MORE DANGER, AND A MAN CALLED ANVIL

Mrs Stine opened the door. When she saw me, her expression changed from harassed to agitated. "Come in," she said. "They want to talk to you." She was already hurrying to the stairs.

"I've told them that I know nothing. They're hoping that you do. It's such a worry."

"What is? Know nothing about what?"

"Oh, dear. I'm not to say."

"Not to say what?"

She was released from the difficulty of trying to work that one out by opening the door of the drawing room and stepping aside. In the room stood Ellen's mother and father and Constable Harty, all looking like the more inquisitive members of the Inquisition.

Constable Harty said, "Ah," as though that explained everything to everyone.

I said, "Is something wrong?"

"There is indeed," Constable Harty replied.

It was clear that he wanted to go through this at slow, steady walking pace. Mrs Charteris didn't. "Ellen is missing," she said. "She left the house very early this morning, before anyone else was up, and she did not return for lunch, which she was expected to do, before accompanying me for the purchase of some new clothes."

"If she has gone somewhere voluntarily, she has probably become engrossed in something. If she has been kidnapped, my immediate suspect would be Patrick Stine."

"And what grounds have you for suspecting him?"

That was a difficult one. The capture of me had not been mentioned to our parents or anyone else at the time, and it would look odd, or just deceitful, to mention it now. And it might interfere with Ellen's plans.

As I hesitated, Constable Harty said, "Just as routine, we have spoken to Mr Stine, and he did tell us that he had to speak sternly to you two girls because you kept spying on him. *I* think that you were very lucky that he left it at that."

That was clever. He had slipped his side of it in first, making it much more realistic with a partial admission. And he had told the Constable, and through him Ellen's parents, that we were spying.

"We weren't spying," I said.

"Well, whatever you call it, it must stop. I'm sure that it's not the sort of thing that your parents and Miss Charteris's parents want to hear you've been doing. And it's certainly not the sort of thing that *we* want to hear you've been doing."

Suddenly, I was very annoyed. "Excuse me," I said. "Aren't we straying from the very much more important matter of Ellen's disappearance."

"Well, perhaps if she hadn't been spying, she wouldn't have disappeared."

With that remark, he upset Mrs Charteris. I added an admonishing look and a shake of my head.

"What do you mean?" Mrs Charteris asked. "What are you suggesting?"

"I'm not suggesting anything."

"Then why did you say it?" I said angrily.

"I," Mrs Charteris said. "shall ask the questions now."

The Constable's smug look immediately vanished when she said, "Then why did you say it?"

"Well, let's just say that children who stay at home and do respectable things are less likely to go missing, and children who go wandering about, spying on people, are more likely to go missing. There are some bad people about in the city."

"Now you alarm me, Constable."

"Oh, no need to be alarmed. I'm not saying that anything bad has happened, or is likely to happen; just that one must never be complacent about the constant dangers that face us all in any large town or city. The river, the canal, carriages, coaches and carts. Just the winding roads and lanes could easily cause someone to become lost. That's probably what has happened."

I couldn't stand any more of his babbling. I said, "I'm going to look for her."

That didn't go down well. Mrs Charteris said, "Joanna. While you are in this house, you are under my protection. I owe it to you and to your parents to refuse permission."

"And I owe it to you and to Ellen to find her!"

They couldn't move as quickly as I could. I ran out of the room, down the stairs and out of the house while they were still thinking about it. A last plea from Mrs Charteris followed me down the stairs like a discarded glove.

This wasn't just a matter of looking for my friend: I was Ellen's assistant, and, in her absence, her deputy. That was how I saw it, and I wasn't in the mood for seeing it in any other way.

When I eventually stopped running, I realised that I didn't know where I was going and didn't know where I *should* go. Even though Mr Stine had to be the main suspect, he wasn't likely to drag Ellen through a busy street and keep her in his room above the butcher's shop. My temporary location had been in the castle ruin in Castle Park. If Ellen had been kidnapped, she could be anywhere. On the other hand, people who kidnapped other people would probably go to check on them, feed them, gloat and so on. It might still be worth watching Mr Stine and following him.

The first problem was that I didn't know where he was. The obvious first place was his room, and the only reasonable course was to stand and watch and wait. I walked to Causewayside, entered by the narrow passage and took up my position beside some convenient bins of rubbish. They were convenient so long as I could tolerate the smell of discarded fish bits. The only relief came from the feebly competing smell of the fishmonger's more or less fresh fish. I had no doubt that it wouldn't be long before I was smelling of fish, too.

Oh, well. This was my duty. I'd do it, no matter how long it took.

It wasn't long.

A hand covered my mouth and another gripped my neck, and I was dragged back into the alley. "Mr Stine expected you," said Torrance. "It really is easy to out-think and predict you brats."

As he talked, in a hissing murmur, he was dragging me back along the passage. "I'll tell you now that Mr Stine has had just about all that he can take of you interfering, pestering brats, and the time has come to punish you, oh, so severely. And I'm going to be part of it. I'm going to ..."

There was a gasp, then a squeal and the hands slid away. As I turned, I saw Torrance go off in a lopsided sort of run to the side of the alley and his head hit the wall. He sank down into a sitting position. His eyes were open, but he seemed to have lost all interest in me.

Well, that was fine up to a point, which was that looming over me was a very large, scruffy and, to be honest, ugly man, who looked, in appearance and in his very recent behaviour, like the sort of man who would knock people on the head and push them into a canal.

He turned away and said, "Come on."

"Where?" I asked nervously. "Who are you?"

He stopped and looked back. "I forgot. Anvil. That's what I'm called. To Ellen."

"Where is she? Have you kidnapped her?"

He groaned. "I've done this in all the wrong order. She warned me about that. Ellen asked me to protect you and to take you to her."

That sounded much better. Ellen was safe and, apparently, still in control of things.

As I should have known.

"Thank you," I said. "That's a relief. Er, lead on, Anvil, and I'll follow."

"Stay close," he said as he set off again.

As I scurried along to keep up with him, I said, "It seems as though everyone guessed what I'd do."

He replied, "Ellen doesn't guess. She … sur … mises."

"Ah."

In the midst of the dark mystery, I had a light mystery. "How do you know Ellen?" I asked.

"Another time," he replied mysteriously.

We had no problem with making our way through the crowded streets because people moved nimbly out of the way of the big man. He turned down a sloping lane, and I saw that we were approaching the docks. When we arrived, I was astonished at the crowded chaos of ships and people, and mountains of stacked crates and bundles; all of it constantly moving, and, it seemed, all of it making noises of grunting, shouting, creaking, shrieking and clumping.

And there, calmly looking out over the water, stood Ellen. If she had been stood in a field or an empty room, she could not have shown less interest in her surroundings.

"Here she is," said Anvil.

Ellen continued to stare, probably at her thoughts. "Hello, Jo," she said. "I'm glad that you're back."

"I nearly wasn't. Your friend saved me."

"Good. When I remembered what I was supposed to be doing today, I anticipated what *my parents* would do, what *you* would do and what *they* would do."

"I'm grateful to you both."

"I have made a decision. With Anvil nearby, we shall visit Mr Stine and try to have a discussion with him."

"Oh. Right. By the way, your parents are very worried and Constable Harty is very annoyed with us for spying on Mr Stine. I think that we ought to go home and do it on another day. We are still bound by duty to our parents."

"You are right, Jo." Ellen sighed. "Anvil. May we call upon you again in a couple of days?"

"Provided that I'm free from work at that time, I shall come with you. It might not be immediate."

"That is understood. Thank you for your help."

"And from me," I added with a smile.

The big man made a slight bow, then ambled away to the crowd of toilers near the ships. As we walked away, Ellen said, "His coming and going is tolerated because his strength is so useful and because he is liked by all, even amongst the roughest workers of the docks. He was a blacksmith, but his reputation for being lenient about payments exceeded his reputation for good quality work. Other people weren't lenient with *him* and his business failed. Now, he works when and where work is available.

"But how do you know him?" I asked.

"While you were away, I could think of nothing better than to walk about, observing. I went by the canal, along the route that he took that night, and I followed people, but that wasn't very helpful because after leaving a public house, most people went into another one. Those who didn't, sat on a bench and went to sleep. Eventually, I came down towards the docks because that is where much crime begins, and ends."

"And that's where you met Anvil?" I prompted.

"Hm? Oh, yes. Well, on the way, I saw two boys playing boisterously. I saw Anvil, giving them a wide berth. One threw a stone at the other, and it went through a shop window. They disappeared in seconds, and when the shopkeeper ran out, and a nearby policeman arrived, there was Anvil and no-one else, except for me, clearly too far away to have had anything to do with it. The indignant shopkeeper assumed that the large and untidy man must have done it, and the policeman agreed. 'Are you going to come quietly?" he asked Anvil hopefully.

'Yes,' Anvil replied.

"Didn't he protest or explain?" I asked.

"No. That is how he thinks, or doesn't think. A policeman had asked him to go quietly; what else was there but to obey? I, however, am made differently. I rushed over and told the shopkeeper and the policeman what had happened. They weren't happy. They had a convenient and docile criminal, and they didn't want to let him go.

'Do you *know* these boys?' the policeman asked, and when I said that I didn't, he sniffed and said, 'I see.'

"It was time to be stern with them. I informed them that if Anvil were to be arrested and charged, I would offer myself as a witness in his defence. Whatever the court's opinion of my quality as a witness might be, at least I had seen the occurrence, which the shopkeeper and the policeman had not."

"You and policemen," I said with a smile.

"They bring it on themselves," she said. "By constantly grabbing at the obvious, they miss what is obvious. I pointed out to them that a man who throws a stone through a shop window either runs away, immediately engages in theft, or gives further vent to whatever injustice has angered him. What he emphatically does *not* do is stand staring while an angry shopkeeper and a policeman arrive to accost him.

'Well, if he didn't do it, why didn't he say so?' the policeman asked, very irritably.

'You did''t ask me,' Anvil replied.

I laughed, but Ellen gently admonished me by holding up a finger and saying, "And that was another error by the policeman, strategic and, I suspect, legal. Having arrived after the window had been broken, and having no grounds for suspecting Anvil, other than his presence, which, as I said, would be unlikely if he had done the thing, he did not ask him, challenge him or even accuse him; he merely asked him whether he was going to go quietly."

"I am impressed. I presume that the policeman wasn't. What happened next?"

"The policeman told Anvil to clear off, and then he told me to clear off, with sundry threats about what would happen to me if he caught me doing anything that I shouldn't be doing. Anvil and I walked away together. For a little while, he said nothing, but as we reached the dock, where he was about to start work, he told me very solemnly that if ever I needed his help, I was just to ask. I received this politely and assured him that he had no reason to consider himself in my debt. He was walking away in one direction, and I was walking away in another, when it occurred to me how useful he could be. I arranged to meet him the next day, before he started work. I told him that he was under no obligation, but that if he wanted to do good things, he could provide valuable assistance to you and me in our investigations."

"I have already seen how valuable he can be."

"That is just a part of it, and not what I was thinking of at first. Jo, we now have someone who can walk into rough public houses and listen. We have someone who works at the dock, who can listen and ask. We have someone who could go without fear to the worst lodging houses in the worst areas and ask questions or look for people. And we have someone who is loyal and dependable and someone to protect us."

"Very valuable indeed."

"I have insisted on paying him what little amount I can afford out of my pocket money. It is the right thing to do, and I don't want him to think that I am just making use of him."

"I'll contribute, too, " I said eagerly. "It's better to pay. We don't want to be asking favours all the time."

"Exactly. Well done. Whatever you can afford."

"It won't be much. It isn't much when it's given to me. But this is much more important and pleasurable than sweets and treats."

"I'm glad you think so. We'll have the rest of today and tomorrow as family normality days; then, I hope, back to it the day after tomorrow. Perhaps we'll make some progress with Mr Stine.

Two days later, we did.

And didn't.

CHAPTER 11

PATRICK STINE WON'T TALK

When I arrived at Ellen's house, she was keen to resume after our little interval. "Presumably," she said as we went along, "it will always be this way. I have no interest in anything else, barely even in food. At least you can close a brain door and shut out the important things while you potter about in your family. I can't. Even though I can't *do*, at least I can think, except for the almost constant interruptions severing the thread of thought."

"I assure you that it is much worse in my family. At least yours are generally absorbed in other things, and are happy to leave you to your own devices. Mine are like a couple of dogs: when they aren't doing things with me, they watch me, waiting for me to do something."

Anvil lived in such a tiny, terraced house that when he opened the door and looked at us, he resembled a tortoise emerging from its shell. But he immediately converted his appearance into that of an excited boy who was going out to play with his best friends. He soon became solemn again when Ellen told him her plan.

"And you want me to stay outside?" he said.

"Outside, but ready to bound up the stairs at a moment's

notice. Jo and I shall stand well apart. An attack on one would produce a yell, or even a scream in Jo's case, from the other."

Slightly ruffled, I said, "You wouldn't scream in an emergency?"

"No. So undignified. Not the thing for a very private detective."

"But all right for the assistant."

"Jo, I'd prefer no screaming by anyone. A firm yell would be sufficient for our loyal protector. However, based on experience, and knowing my own preferences and methods, I consider it much more likely that you would scream than I. On the other hand, you are just as likely to stand still and say, "Excuse me. I'd very much prefer it if you wouldn't hurt my friend."

"Oh, Ellen!"

The very private detective condescended to wink at me.

The conversation ended as we entered Causewayside. "No sign of the guard," Ellen said.

"Perhaps he saw Anvil."

"In that case, one would expect him to hurry across the road and go and tell Stine, which he didn't unless he was very quick. We shall soon see."

The three of us walked boldly to the stairs next to the butcher shop. Ellen nodded at Anvil and we went up the stairs and knocked on the only door on the small landing. After three knocks and no reply, Ellen, never one to be deterred by minor obstacles, turned the handle. The door opened.

"Mr Stine?" Ellen called, with the door only slightly open. She opened it a bit more, then drew in her breath and said, "Ah. I didn't expect that."

Following her into the room, I saw what she had seen. On the floor, his head in a pool of dried blood, lay Mr Patrick Stine. A whirl of partly-formed thoughts swirled round my head. Who? Why? What did it mean? What were we to do next?"

The immediate next was controlled by Ellen. "We must look for things," she said. "Walk very carefully, over there, or stand still. At least we have the body this time."

"Ellen," I said. "This is a dead man. It isn't one of those complicated puzzles."

"That's exactly what it is," she replied. "It just happens to have real people in it."

"And real murders."

"Yes. I know it isn't pleasant, but that should be an incentive to solve this and bring the killer, or killers, to justice. What we must do here, first, is to find clues as to the assailant's identity. Then, here and elsewhere, we must look for the assailant's motive. This wasn't a drunken brawl. He wasn't attacked in an alley. Someone entered his room and attacked him … from the back."

As she was speaking, she was thinking and looking across the room. "The murderer might have asked for a drink, just to make the victim turn away, or he might have asked for money, or a document, or a photograph, or …"

"A diamond?"

"That's tight, JO. That's what I'm hoping. We don't know, but Stine was definitely attacked from behind, although, hmm, the wounds are at the front."

Although the dead man had fallen on his front, he had conveniently turned his head, showing both his face and a deep wound to his temple, and another in the middle of his forehead. I was willing to take Ellen's word about the wounds. I wasn't going to look. The presence of a dead person, and a murdered one at that, was quite enough for me.

I looked across the room as Ellen was doing. There was a bookcase, which I wasn't surprised to see didn't contain any books. Ellen walked quickly over to it and looked at the top shelf. "Aha," she said, pleased, and swung round to face me, eyes blazing.

"As you would expect, Mr Stine was not one for dusting

his furniture, which is why the bookcase has a thick layer of dust on it. Except for one square, where there is less dust, and four very small circles where there is no dust."

"Although I didn't follow the details, I understood her point. "Something was there and has been moved?" I suggested.

"Not just something. There is slight dust at the edges of the square and there are four, *four*, round points in which there is no dust, which suggests …."

"Ah. A box?"

"Yes. A box on four small legs. *Now!*"

She scurried back to the body and looked closely at it, without touching it, and all around it. She straddled it, staring at the wounds. She went on her knees and peered at the linoleum floor; then, still not touching, she looked very carefully at the clothes, putting her head down to the floor, as though trying to see under the body.

I guessed that she was trying to ascertain what Stine had been doing when he was struck, but she baffled me by quickly standing and going to the window and peering at it from several angles. After that, she studied the floor, stooped over, walking slowly back to the door. And finally, she stood and looked all around the room.

"The visitor was not expected," she said. "He suddenly opened the door and entered. Stine rushed to the window, wondering why Torrance had not at least warned him. We'll come back to that. There might have been a brief discussion, but probably not. In either case, Stine began to dash across the room in order to grab and protect his box. The murderer grabbed him from behind, Stine slipped and fell with the assailant on him. With that weight on his back, he banged his head on the hard floor. That might have made him groggy, but the assailant made sure by banging his head again on the floor, making a second and deeper wound. It is probable that murder wasn't intended, that the killer wanted only to prevent interference while he removed whatever it was."

When I shook my head in amazement, Ellen said, "I am surmising, of course. I am making some small assumptions based on such things as marks on the floor and making a guess about the window. But that is fine, so long as it doesn't prevent our seeing things that indicate otherwise. It is a framework. It might be wrong in some of the details, but I think that broadly it provides an accurate account of what happened."

"I can follow that," I said, "but I am having difficulty putting it all together; this death, the other Stine's death, the eagerness of this Stine to blame the other Stine's son, while apparently possessing something of great importance and perhaps relevance."

I stopped, a little embarrassed about this unusual verbosity, but Ellen tipped her head in approval. "Excellent, Jo. You have neatly summed up the knot which we must untie. I assure you that I don't have it clear in my head yet, but it is forming. Think back to Robert's statement. The hospital and the ship."

"Ah," I gasped. "So, Leonard and Patrick were both killed for the diamond. By the mystery man, or by another one who wants it?"

"That is what we must work out. Amongst the sort of company that the Stines kept, the mere mention of a large diamond would attract a lot of people who would not be very reluctant to commit murder. Let's not rule out Torrance Kiddle, or someone working on his behalf. Let's not rule out … anyone."

From downstairs came Anvil's voice, asking for confirmation that all was well. Ellen reassured him and we went down to him. Ellen explained briefly and suggested that it would be best for him to return to his work or home, rather than to be so close to the scene of a murder. "Large labouring men seem always to be high on the list of suspects," she said.

"Especially in such a case as this, where strength was required."

Anvil nodded his agreement, but he wasn't keen to leave us. "Anvil," Ellen said, almost sternly, "we shall need you often for protection, and for your knowledge and your familiarity with the ways of your part of the city. I don't want to force you into being a permanent protector as we go about doing our investigating. We shall be fine. Thank you again for your help."

When he had left, Ellen was keen to search behind the shop, but I was keen to avoid our being suspects when the dead body was discovered. She agreed. She looked round, but all the city policemen had disappeared, or had concealed themselves effectively. She shrugged and went into the butcher's shop.

When she came out, a couple of minutes later, she said, "He wasn't pleased. His lodger has been murdered, and now it is his responsibility to report the death. And we still haven't bought anything."

We crossed the road, and slightly separated as we searched in the dark parts of the passage, looking in the heaps of rubbish. A couple of bodies turned out to be sleeping men, and there was no sign of Torrance.

"Therefore," Ellen said, "it is reasonable to suppose that, for whatever reason, Torrance was not here. That might mean that my surmising was not entirely correct, and Torrance wasn't expected to be here. It might be because he had some other duties which entailed his temporary absence. It might be because he was instructed, perhaps paid, by someone to be elsewhere. And it might be that he killed Mr Stine, or at least caused his death. It would be very helpful to know where he is."

Abruptly, she went back across Causewayside and into the butcher's shop. Out on the pavement, I heard his protest at her reappearance.

"No!" he shouted. "I don't know anything about any friends of his. Now, clear off and leave me alone. And if you've any sense, which I doubt, you'll clear off, too. I've sent a boy to fetch a policeman."

"That's fine," Ellen said, assuming her soothing voice.. "You have our names and addresses. We have nothing to hide and don't want you to bear all the burden of this terrible thing. I was curious about that unpleasant person, and wondered what his connection was."

Somewhat mollified, the butcher said, "Well, all right, yes, I know the one that you mean. That feckless thing that used to hang around him, used to irritate me, doing all that watching from across the way. I think he lived farther down. I might have seen him go into one of the buildings, no idea which one, about a hundred yards that way."

"Thank you," Ellen said. "You have been very helpful. If you should have any trouble with the policeman, just refer him to me."

It was difficult to imagine Ellen in a classroom again.

"Did you hear?" she asked when she came out.

"Yes. A stroll along Causewayside?"

"Yes."

It wasn't a pleasant stroll. Causewayside was one of those ways with one end which is far superior to the other, with a gradual, then steady, deterioration in between. The small businesses became smaller and scruffier: a pawn shop, a tripe shop, a shop which seemed to sell nothing but rags; then, as though giving up, they stopped, and both sides consisted of tall, and small, leaning and crumbling terraced houses. Ragged children played or squatted on steps or on the kerb, where there was a kerb, the pavement in places having sunk into the road. Small groups of men leaned against walls, smoking, spitting, sharing muttered comments. As we passed, they all glanced suspiciously. And there were other dark looks that I didn't like. It was enough to make me want to turn and walk quickly back and away from Causewayside. Of course, Ellen walked over to one of the groups and said, "Hello. We're looking for Torrance. Do you know where he is?"

There was some shaking of heads and twisting of lips to imply that they had not heard of him. But someone from a nearby group called, "Why do you want him?"

"We have a job for him." Ellen was always thinking ahead, anticipating questions, ready with the answers, always already in her role. "He works for an acquaintance of ours, Patrick Stine. He said that Torrance might be available and willing for the right price."

Would they *really* believe that?

Yes, because Ellen had absolute confidence in herself. There was some looking, raising and lowering of eyebrows, then some shrugging. "Number 96, second floor," the man from the other group said.

"Thanks," Ellen said. "Much appreciated. Come on, Jo."

I was pleased with her success, but I wasn't pleased about walking into the dark and dingy hall of the indicated house. For one thing, there was the possibility of a trap. There was also the possibility of one man peeling away from his group and following us, for one of many possible, horrible, reasons. However, being Ellen's assistant, I said nothing and followed the leader up the creaking stairs, trying not to faint as I breathed the ghastly odours of the place.

On the first landing, there was one door and a corridor with other doors. It was easy to see that it had once been a large house with a lot of character, before death or poverty had provided the opportunity for the conversion into a large number of apartments. Ellen knocked on the first door.

"Who is it?" called a gratey voice after some shuffling about.

Ellen didn't bother with asking whether Torrance lived there. Either he did or he didn't.

Being vague would arouse suspicion. She called through the door, "Mrs Kiddle, Mr Stine wants Torrance for a job."

"Well, who are you?"

"Messengers for Mr Stine. He told us to fetch his friend Torrance."

"That man is no friend of my Torrance. He just makes use of him."

"Well, he wants to make use of him again."

"He isn't here."

"Where is he?"

"I don't know, and I'd not tell the likes of you, dragging him into bad ways."

Ellen murmured to me, "I doubt that he needed much dragging." Aloud, she said, "Did he tell you that he might be working for Mr Stine today?"

"Not that I recall. He doesn't tell me all his business."

"I'd very much prefer to discuss this with you inside, rather than shout for all the neighbourhood to hear. We have already aroused much curiosity. There is no need to be afraid. We'll step back and you peep. We are two girls."

We stepped away, and the door slowly opened. Two eyes blinked at us. The door opened a little more and the head emerged and looked to the right and the left. "Come in, then," the woman said.

Bad as the air was on the stairs, on entering the room I wanted to rush back out. It was one room, with a sink and a stove behind a curtain. It wasn't a large room, and it was made much smaller by an array of beds and cribs, all in disarray and all stinking. There were seven sniffing, snuffling babies that I could see.

Mrs Kiddle was small and prematurely aged, her son's age making her no more than forty, but she looked at least sixty, and a badly-kept sixty at that. Her hair was grey from age and dirt, as though her daily work were cleaning out the ashes from all the grates of the city. Her wrinkles made her look as though she were in the same drying process that turns a grape into a raisin. Her eyes were blank, except for the minor illumination of mistrust. Of what? Everything, I expect.

"Now," she said. "What have two girls to do with my son, except leading him into bad ways and worse ways?"

"As I said, we're messengers. We run errands. Pennies come in handy when you're poor."

"Do you think I don't know that?" Mrs Kiddle snarled. "I've been poor a lot longer than you. That's why I take in babies. I have to earn money somehow."

Ellen took a deep breath, then clearly regretted it. I knew that she was controlling herself, concentrating on the purpose of this conversation.

The woman peered at her, and me. "You don't *look* poor. Those look like nice clothes."

"We don't waste our pennies on cheap pleasures," Ellen replied. "We save them. And we have more than one employer."

"Save? *I* can't afford to save."

Ellen's glance said clearly that she didn't want to prolong this. "Mrs Kiddle, your son was supposed to be working for Mr Stine today, providing an observational service."

"You mean keeping watch for him."

"Yes. I'm glad that you understand that, and have expressed it plainly. Your expectation being the same as ours, you will share our surprise to know that your son was not performing that task earlier today, and that Mr Stine has been killed."

"You said...."

"I lied. I needed this conversation. Stine has been killed, not long after his brother was killed."

"Killed? Well, don't you try blaming it on my boy."

"We have no intention of doing that, Mrs Kiddle. Please understand my point. Your son was observing for Mr Stine, standing on guard. Mr Stine has been killed. What we now want to know is, first, where your son is; secondly, whether your son, or you, know of any other acquaintances, or enemies, of Mr Stine?"

"Most people who knew that man were his enemies. He'd have had no friends. But I didn't know any of them, friends or foes."

"What about work connections? What was his work?"

"Skullduggery. Debt collection. Revenge. Anything that needed a strong arm and no conscience. That's why I wanted my boy to keep well away."

"The sooner that we talk to your boy, the better. Where does he go when he isn't here or patrolling for Stine?"

"Oh, well, I don't pry. I respect his privacy. He goes for walks, meets his friends."

"Where? Where does he meet these friends?"

"*I* don't know. I'm only his mother. He comes home for his meals, a change of clothes, and most nights to sleep, but I don't interfere with him."

"Mrs Kiddle. Your son wasn't at his post, opposite Stine's room. If Stine wanted him to be there, that is where he would have been. But he wasn't. That implies that he was persuaded to leave or was removed. Now, Stine was a strong and vicious man, but he is now dead. We, you, need to know what has happened to your son."

"Do you think he's been harmed?"

"It is possible. He has been doing jobs for a bad man who has a powerful enemy."

"There's a kitchen in St Mark's, where he goes. He did tell me that. He plays cards, sits by the fire, drinks tea and eats sausages. A bit like a club. And of course, he visits an occasional beer place. The Spread Eagle is one."

"Thank you, Mrs Kiddle."

"If you find him, you'll tell him that I'm worried about him, and want him to come home?"

"Of course."

Outside, the lounging men stared at us, wondering what our business really was. I looked away and wanted to depart quickly, but Ellen stopped and stared back at the men in both groups.

"What?" one of the men asked.

"Two men have been killed, and Torrance Kiddle is missing. There has already been evasion in your responses. I am now looking in your faces for indications that you were involved."

"You load of impudence! You'd better clear off before some of us forget we're decent people."

"Oh, I don't think you were involved. Torrance Kiddle was clearly involved with clever criminals such as Patrick Stine. Not your sort of business."

There were immediate snorts of contempt, and the angry man said, "Patrick Stine? A clever criminal? He was just the debt collector, and arranger. He just did as he was told."

"Oh, yes? By whom?"

Ellen dangled just enough doubt to draw him out, but as he began to speak, one of his companions cuffed him on the back of the head, saying, "He might be annoyed if he knew that you'd said his name."

"Aye, you're right," said the angry man.

"Well, thanks anyway," Ellen said, and we walked away with that calm confidence that was settling into me, too.

At a safe distance, Ellen said, "What did you hear before he was interrupted?"

"St... That was all. Steven? Stuart? Stanley?"

"Perhaps Stanley Chissing, the owner of the Spread Eagle Inn. His name is over the door."

"Leonard Stine's last place of drinking."

"Yes. And where Torrance Kiddle goes. I think it's time for our large friend to be of assistance again."

CHAPTER 12

ANVIL SETS A TRAP

"No!"

Even Ellen was shocked to see, and hear, Anvil being stern almost to the point of fiery.

"But there might be developments."

"They'll keep. I won't have you waiting in the darkness, near the canal and that place. And that's an end of it."

He folded his arms and looked away. I smiled at Ellen. Without quite smiling, she made a small gesture of acceptance. "Very well, Anvil. The children will go home and leave the big grown-up to do the interesting stuff."

Anvil nodded. "I'll do a quick visit in the middle of the day, then spend a few hours there in the evening, watching and listening."

"*Just* watching and listening, Anvil. Don't be tempted into anything dangerous. At all times, put your own safety before anything else."

"I shall."

"And thank you again. We are very grateful.

"Always happy to help. I'll report to you tomorrow."

He did, and it was very interesting.

During the day, the Spread Eagle Inn came close to being respectable, with a steady coming and going of labouring men, for most of whom it was no more than a convenient place in which to quench their thirst.

For the main part, these were more or less honest people. Some betting was done, mostly through gestures and looks; the conversation was that of rough men who were not constrained by the presence of women or children; and some, still sweating and dirty from their work in foundry, factory or mill, wanted only to wash away the heat and dirt with several glasses of beer.

In the early evening, this continued, but as the evening became night, there was a gradual change, leading to the sudden awareness that the change was complete. By nine o'clock, Anvil realised that he was standing in a dense crowd in which every corruption was represented by at least one person.

Anvil's slowness of thought was the result of his low opinion of himself. Alone, and with an important task for his special friend, he was as shrewd and alert as anyone, and more than anyone, in the Inn. He was careful to confine his visual observation to casually peripheral glances, while seeming to have all his attention on his beer.

Listening, he heard much discussion of illegal and immoral matters, and much business was done in mutters and growls. But there was nothing that seemed to have any bearing on the recent occurrences.

The hours slid by. Anvil drank slowly, but tried not to be suspiciously, or irritatingly, slow. Fortunately, he had been paid recently and he wasn't easily affected by beer, especially the beer in the Spread Eagle, which he had no doubt had been watered.

The Spread Eagle Inn wasn't one of those places with a jug and bottle; children and beshawled old women waited at the back with their jugs and other receptacles for beer to take home. It had one large room, in which men, and only men, drank, generally until they ran out of money, or were so intoxicated that they were removed from the premises and propelled, with no attempt at accuracy or moderation, towards the path beside the canal. Fortunately for the intoxicated ones, their control of their legs was so feeble that they rarely reached even the path.

Between the arrival of a customer and that man's lack of money or lack of ability to consume any more beer, Stanley Chissing was as helpful and encouraging as anyone could be. When you reached the point at which your pockets were empty or your body was full and overflowing, which you reached with his hearty encouragement, he had no further use for you and desired your company no more.

Guided by the same principle, Stanley Chissing permitted no fighting in, or very near, his inn, on the grounds that it interrupted those who were already drinking and discouraged those who were intending to enter and consume. But many appointments were made for meetings at certain nearby locations for the settling of disputes. It was a place of violence, but violence deferred and relocated.

But as the evening became night, and the night became late night, and there were few departures, Anvil began to wonder about the full name of the place. Was this still an inn? Or was it just one of those names that persist long after the changed use of a place? When he bought his next pint of beer, he asked.

"Is this an inn in name or in function?"

It was Stanley Chissing who had served him, Anvil having chosen carefully the moment in which to thrust out his arm and call for service. Stanley Chissing looked at him with distaste.

"Do you mean do we put people up?"

"Yes."

"Well, talk simple in future. Right, then. Would that be a bed in a room on your own, a bed in a room to be shared, or a bed on any bit of floor on which we can fit a couple of blankets?"

"On my own. It must be on my own."

"Ah. Don't like people?"

"Don't trust people."

"My guests are all respectable and well-behaved. I insist on it."

"Everyone can be tempted, and many give way. I have a special reason for wanting to be anonymous and unnoticed for a couple of days while I make my arrangements. I don't interfere with other people, and I expect the same from them."

"Well, it's all live and let live here."

"Someone didn't let Leonard Stine live."

"That had nothing to do with my customers."

Anvil leaned forward. "I know all about that, and I know why."

Stanley Chissing tried to be nonchalant. "Oh? Why?"

Anvil tapped his nose. "Never mind. Let's just say that it's one reason for wanting to be out of the way for a little while, in a place where I can trust the owner. Now, do you have a room?"

"How many nights?"

"Possibly a couple, depending on how my arrangements go."

First, the pretence. "This is a very respectable house. I don't want its reputation to be ruined by a pack of policemen demanding admission in their pursuit of you."

"No. Nothing like that. The police don't suspect me. No problem with them. Someone has it fixed in his head that I killed someone and stole something."

"He must have some reason."

Anvil shrugged, settling into his new character. "Let's all mind our own business, eh?

The landlord's eyes gave Anvil a clear view of what was happening in his brain. After a few moments, Chissing said, "Wait there and I'll find out what's available."

Anvil saw through the pretence. He saw suppressed excitement. He watched the arrangement being made with a couple of the drinkers. Their immediate response was annoyance, but as the matter was explained, they glanced at Anvil, then nodded.

"Yes, that's all arranged," Chissing said. "Just had to do a bit of reorganising. Right. That's two shillings a night, payable in advance, just in case your arrangements take you away rather too quickly for such minor matters as paying your bill."

He provided what he thought was a pleasant smile. It was a horrible mixture of teeth, lips and cunning. Anvil smiled back. "Fair enough," he said.

"It's nothing fancy, of course," added Mr Chissing.

"Of course," agreed Anvil. "A bed and privacy is all that I need. And a good night's sleep."

"Sleep well, do you?" The landlord tried to sound lightly conversational. Anvil almost grinned. He understood.

"Oh, yes. No problems on that score. When I'm out, I'm well out. And I've had a tiring few days."

"Another pint?"

"One more. Then I'll turn in and have some of that refreshing sleep."

The beer was drunk. Anvil went out the back for necessaries, then used a candle to go up the rickety stairs to his room. There was no-one to assist, but the house wasn't large, and the landlord's instructions were clear.

"Hmm," murmured Anvil when he opened the bedroom door. He was used to simple and scruffy, but not filthy. Something scuttled under the bed and scrabbled into one of the walls. It was a good thing that Anvil didn't want that deep sleep with which he had baited Mr Chissing. Well, he thought, it was a bright idea, but he wasn't looking forward to long hours of sitting on his bed in this room, waiting for whatever was going to happen.

He sat down on the bed, with his back to the walls, and as soon as the bed had stopped its spring symphony, he settled down to wait.

For a moment, he closed his eyes, and immediately fell asleep.

Anvil had lied about being a deep sleeper, but when he heard the creaking and whispering outside his room, he was annoyed with himself for having slept at all. He was relieved to find that he was still in the sitting position. Being on his back would have put him at a considerable disadvantage. He lowered his head, then carefully lowered his eyelids like a couple of doors, ready to peep through the thin crack that remained at the lower portions of his visitors.

The door slowly opened. In trying to avoid creaking hinges, the intruders opened the door a little bit at a time, which produced a series of short, sharp creaks instead of one long one. There were two of them. One held a long knife, the other a crowbar. They slowly walked into the room, taking up their positions, one slightly to the left, the other slightly to the right. The strategy was clear: one would go for the throat, and in the event of difficulty, the other would swing the crowbar. Anvil sighed inwardly. Once again, he was going to have to use his great strength against people instead of for work. But he had manoeuvred them into this. They were here, as it were, at his bidding.

As the knife approached, Anvil's hand gripped the wrist. His body surged forward and he gripped the other man's wrist. When Anvil gripped a wrist, there was always an excellent reason, from which had developed his custom of squeezing until important parts of the wrist cracked. The men howled and flapped at Anvil with their other arms. The result was more crackings. The knife and the crowbar fell to the floor. Anvil twisted and with further howls and gasps of pain, the men sank to their knees.

"Now," Anvil said. "I know *you*, Torrance Kiddle. What is *your* name?"

"Lucas MacReady. We were just following orders, and the weapons were just for protection. We were hoping not to have to use them."

"With the blade at my throat? Right. You didn't want to use your weapons on me. What did you intend to do?"

Hesitation.

Squeeze and twist.

Crunching and crackling.

Howls and yelps.

"Milsom!" cried Torrance Kiddle, glancing towards the door, where a large, scowling man stood looking in at them. Another man stood beside him, not appearing fully because of the other man's bulk.

Anvil looked down at the crowbar, then back at the big man. The man thought for a few seconds, sniffed, said, "Nah," and walked away, leaving the intruders to their fate.

It was time for another squeeze and twist.

"Aaaaggghhh. We were just looking for any money or valuables. Honest."

It was feasible, but not when you connected everything. Anvil applied some more persuasion.

"Aaaaaggghhh. Okay, okay. We were told you had something valuable."

"What?"

"None of your business," said Stanley Chissing. He was standing in the doorway, pointing a pistol at Anvil. "Let go of those men and clear off out of here. And don't come..."

He was interrupted by the sudden arrival, through what air there was, of Torrance Kiddle, flung like a rag by Anvil. As the helpless Kiddle collided with the landlord, knocking down his arm, the gun went off and there was a scream. Anvil was right behind Torrance and he grabbed Stanley Chissing and pulled him into the room, then applied the same disarming technique on the wrist, with the same success. He was relieved to see that Torrance had been shot in the leg. Torrance seemed not to be relieved as he writhed about, yelping and groaning. Lucas MacReady was hissing and groaning over his wrist with that selfish preoccupation that comes over people at such times.

Looking down with disgust at the cowardly villains, Anvil knew that he would rather spend the rest of the night in a pig sty than anywhere near these people. In his hurry, he gave the landlord's wrist such a squeeze and twist that the desired information poured out like blood from a deep wound.

"A diamond," Chissing gasped. "Len Stine stole it from someone. I don't know who had it before he did. He wouldn't say. Len was killed for it. I don't know who did it. It might have been his brother. I don't know who killed his brother. You seemed to have something to do with the diamond. It seemed worth having a look."

"Leonard Stine told you about the diamond?"

"He wanted credit for more beer."

"In a place like this, his fate would have been sealed."

"He'd been in other places. He might have showed it in one of those, and then been followed."

"That's true. Right. I've had enough of this place for one night. I might be back to ask questions again. In the meantime, you come down with me and return my money."

The landlord thought about protesting, but Anvil's size and strength and, he had to admit, the circumstances, combined to produce a sensible response. "Follow me," he said.

In the bar, a couple of small candles smeared a pale yellow light over the darkness. Anvil saw an occasional smudge of a face, like a careless fingerprint on a dirty sheet. He could feel the watching eyes, the animosity. He stood and looked round, letting the watchers know that he had no fear of them. It wasn't necessary. They had heard and seen.

Anvil took his money, gave the injured and bitter landlord a final look of warning, then slid the bolts and left.

Outside, he paused briefly. This was one of those parts of the city that sank into the darkness of the night like a stone dropped in a black swamp. Many men went into the canal without any assistance from murderers. He worked out where the path was and slowly followed it At the top of the steps, he set off towards the pale glow of a distant gas lamp, beginning his slow walk home.

Well, he reassured himself as he went along, he'd done what he'd set out to do.

CHAPTER 13

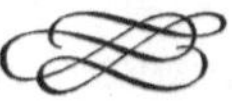

MORE PROGRESS

Ellen was delighted with Anvil's progress. "Our short version of the sequence of events now has a diamond at the beginning and at the end. Anvil, no more risks, please. But I think this case is moving towards its conclusion."

She ignored his protests as she handed over our combined amount of money. "We don't want favours, pity or any other form of justification. We want you as a worker for our cause, and we want it to be a long association. And I might speak to you shortly about what I hope will be the last task, until the next time. Therefore, we shall pay you for your services."

With frowns and sighs, he accepted the money. Then, he went back to work.

"What are *we* going to do?" I asked.

"We are going to go to the police station."

"Oh. What are we going to do there?"

"I am hoping to be given some crucial information."

Once more, off we went, Ellen leading and I following. I was right beside her, but definitely following.

As you would expect, no-one at the police station was pleased to see us. The sternly disapproving looks began as soon as we entered. The disapproval quickly rose as Ellen talked.

"I wish to review the case against Mr Robert Stine," she said. "What is happening?"

"What's that to do with you?" the sergeant said, making his thick moustache, that necessary policeman's appendage, quiver with his indignation.

"For one thing, I am a member of the public, which pays for your employment and the services which you provide. Secondly, I am closely connected with Mr Stine's mother. She is my parent's housekeeper. Thirdly, I am investigating this case."

"Well," said the sergeant. "Here's your review. Stine is in prison and staying there. As for the rest, mind your own business and go and play with dolls or knit, or whatever girls do these days to pass the time."

"*This* girl investigates murder cases. You are clearly going to be of no assistance. Very likely you are not involved with any more complicated aspect than the documentation. I desire an interview with Detective Mellor."

The sergeant raised an arm that quivered like a spear and pointed to the door. "Out!" he bellowed.

"Don't be absurd," Ellen said. "You are an official with the responsibility to protect the public, not order them about when they request assistance, especially when *I* expect to assist *you*."

I supported Ellen with some enthusiastic nodding.

"Detective Mellor is out and won't be back for several hours." He said it with a triumphant finality as though that were his other way of firmly concluding the matter.

"We'll wait," Ellen replied.

We sat on a wooden bench beneath the window. The sergeant tried to look very busy and not at all bothered by our presence. I knew that Ellen was propped up by stubbornness, but I soon began to droop. I suspected that this was a battle of wills between Ellen and the sergeant, and the prospect of sitting on a hard seat for several hours was not appealing. I was even on the verge of whispering to Ellen that perhaps we should come back later, when a door opened and Detective Mellor strode out.

"Sergeant," he said. "Let me have the initial report on the warehouse robbery."

The sergeant tried to bluff by ignoring us. "Yes, sir. It's right here, sir."

Ellen rose from her seat and approached the detective from the side. "Detective Mellor," she said. "I'm so pleased to see you. The sergeant told us that you were out and not expected back for several hours."

"She wouldn't take no for an answer," the sergeant explained.

"That's all right. You did the right thing. I don't have time to waste on schoolgirls."

"The sergeant will be called to confirm in court that you refused to receive vital information in the case of the murder of Leonard Stine."

"Very well. What is your vital information?"

"Has a large diamond been stolen from a shop or person in the last few months?"

"That, little girl, is not information; it is a question."

"The answer to the question will provide the information."

"You are very annoying."

"Of course. I am efficient and making excellent progress on this case, whereas you appear to be making none. Now, I don't recall any newspaper reports of the theft of a large diamond. Do you know of any?"

"No."

"Then, there is your information."

"Have you made *any* progress? What about the death of Patrick Stine? That wasn't Robert Stine's doing. He was here, with you. So, what have you been doing since arresting and charging the wrong man?" She looked at each man inturn.

"Come, Jo. I have my crucial information. It's time to finish this."

We walked quickly out, leaving the two policemen standing, I presumed, with mouths hanging open, then reverting to their customary scowls, to the inevitable accompaniment of mutterings about irritating and insolent schoolgirls.

Not wanting to admit that I didn't know what was going on, I said, "What next?"

"To the booking office," she replied.

At the docks, we went to the booking office, waited patiently for our turn, then approached the clerk.

Ellen went straight into what she had prepared. "My father was injured in the war in Kurukhstan. His brother is hoping to come home soon on a civilian ship. When is the next one due?"

"Whoo," the clerk exhaled. "Have a seat. There aren't many, and probably nothing direct. This could take a while, and I must keep serving people."

"That's fine," Ellen said. "It would be helpful, too, to know when the next one will go the other way, and when the previous one went."

Another exhalation and a sniff. The clerk began to consult ledgers and rustle through papers, being interrupted frequently by customers. But after a while, he called Ellen over and said, "As I said, not many, nothing goes straight there, except troops and supplies. Here, write these down and that will give you all you need to know."

He passed a couple of open ledgers across to Ellen, pointed in the direction of the relevant entries and served another customer. Very pleased with her progress, Ellen wrote down the information that she wanted. Before we left, she checked one more thing with the clerk.

"Well, yes," he said. "Just as you can go by any one of a dozen ways from here to wherever you live, so someone could make that journey as slow and as complicated as he wanted. Some people like to take in some other countries on their way to anywhere. They make a big tour of it."

"And if I were trying to evade pursuers, it would suit me to travel that way."

"Well, now, that's an interesting way for a young girl to be looking at things, but yes, I suppose that it could be an effective strategy. On the other hand, that lengthens the time in which you might be caught."

"Indeed it does. And if you were carrying something valuable, it would increase the opportunities for thieves." She gave the clerk a respectful nod. "You have been very helpful. Thank you."

"You're welcome," replied the clerk, who was one of those people who derive pleasure from doing their job well, and additional pleasure from doing additional things.

As we left the booking office, Ellen glanced at the calendar on the wall and noted the date.

Outside, there was a rumble and a shout of "Mind yourselves!" A trolley loaded with crates, pulled by a man at the front and pushed by a man at the back, passed just in front of us. All around was bustle and heaving and clumping and clattering and hooting and shouting. The ships stood aloofly beside all this noisy work, their naked masts rising above it all like symbols of their disdain.

The ships had brought their cargoes over the turbulent seas; all that these people had to do was move the stuff from one place to another, on firm, safe ground.

Ellen knew that all this was not only interesting, but stimulating, even exciting, but she was very skilled at separating the responses and involvement of her senses from her thinking, and keeping the task clearly in view. This she did now, looking through all the activity for the big man who was such a valuable assistant. Even amongst all the strong men and crates, boxes and sacks, he was easy to find. He came over to Ellen as soon as he had a few seconds. He didn't waste time with questions, but raised his head slightly, inviting her to tell him what she wanted.

"Thursday morning at seven o'clock. Departures." she said. "The Eglantine."

"I'll be there," he said and immediately returned to his work.

When she arrived at my house, we put on a short display of discussing other matters in order to lull my parents. When they had moved away, Ellen said, "An early start on Thursday. I'll collect you at half past six. We're going to look at the ships."

"I suppose that you don't want to tell me why."

"That's right. I might be wrong. I might be right *and* wrong. And I think that you should do a little working out for yourself."

She waited impatiently while I sought the permission of my parents to go off at that time.

"Why so early?" Mother asked.

"Because some ships sail on the early tide, and we want to watch them leave."

Ellen had been hovering, listening. "Well done," she whispered as I went with her to the door. "I'll see you at half past six." Her eyes gleamed as she added, "It might be a very interesting day."

CHAPTER 14

ELLEN DOES IT

I admit that I am not at my sharpest first thing in the morning. I don't stagger about, yawning, but I am not at my best. Ellen was annoyingly lively, very impatient when I hesitated, dropped things and went back for things. When we eventually set off, at a very brisk place, she said, "If I'd known how slow you are, I'd have suggested collecting you at six o'clock."

I'd have made a sharp retort, but I was too sleepy.

After we had gone a little way, I said, "It would be nice to have an idea of what we are going to do."

"Yes, it would," she agreed. "Please excuse my reticence. I am aware that I might be completely wrong about this. Admitting failure would be bad enough without first raising expectations."

"I understand. But don't expect me to respond quickly in a crisis when I don't even know that there is a crisis."

"I'm hoping that there won't be anything for you to do. But I like to have my assistant with me, and I thought that you'd like to be involved."

"Thank you. Yes, I do like to be involved."

"Good."

We continued to walk at a brisk pace, and I was having to scuttle in order to keep up with Ellen's long strides. She showed no signs of hurrying, but she moved quickly and steadily along.

With the help of some unexpected short cuts along lanes and passages which I hadn't even known were there, we were soon at the docks. Then, it was a matter of finding our precise destination and going to it, without being crushed or trampled, or merely knocked out of the way. It was only as Ellen searched for the spot that she wanted that I became aware of how big the docks were. A further surprise was the chaos of ships, shoving, bumping, hooting and creaking, making the whole area a Regent Street on water.

"That's what we want," Ellen announced, pointing across a right-angled turn, where three large steamships stood looking away from the boisterous delivery and collection of cargoes. The great warehouses were replaced by low sheds. There were still plenty of people and plenty of large boxes, but these were clearly travellers and their luggage. But even this wasn't our precise destination. Beyond the three large steamships, hidden by their bulk, was a much smaller one which seemed to be performing every nautical task: fish were being unloaded, crates were being loaded, bags of luggage were being hauled up planks and there were busy, flustered clerks and passengers milling about the quay.

"Now," said Ellen, "we must try to be inconspicuous."

"Two girls, wandering about a busy dock?"

"Inconspicuous rather than a danger to someone. Let us look at the ships."

"I prefer the ships with sails. I don't like these noisy, smelly things. The bullies of the sea."

"Greater speed and efficiency will always seem ugly. Not at all what we want, until we make a journey and want to do it in half the time or less, and with much less chance of being wrecked. The train was very unpopular until people realised the benefit to themselves."

"People are selfish."

"Of course. But in a few hours, those fish will be sold, relatively fresh, in markets and shops, in towns and cities many miles from here."

I knew that she was right, and I went into a deep ponder about efficiency and convenience against beauty and rhythm, and I wondered to what it would all lead.

"We are early," Ellen said. "You are welcome to look around. I am too tense. We might be almost at the climax. I shall stand and watch, and be ready and alert."

"I shall wait with you."

"In that case, please try to look as though you are not waiting with me."

I turned and stared at the nearby ships, trying to look as though everything was deeply interesting. Actually, apart from the hull and the sails, I had little idea of anything that I could see. It all looked like a very complicated mess of tangled ropes, baskets, crates and tools, through and over which people stepped awkwardly or crawled, like large flies on coils of seaweed.

With a strange detachment, I was about to go for a closer look when Ellen said, "Ah. I think that this is the one."

She left my side and walked to intercept a man who was walking quickly towards the small ship.

"Mr Iqbal," she called. "May I speak with you?"

The man turned and looked at her with a puzzled, worried expression and said, "I am in a great hurry."

"The ship will leave at the set time. There is time for a brief discussion."

"No. I have things to attend to before I sail."

"So have I."

"Very well. What do you want?"

"Mr Iqbal, I want you to do the decent and honourable thing, and prevent the execution of an innocent man."

Mr Iqbal's eyes widened and his mouth followed suit. But he quickly covered his shock and dismay."

"I don't know what you mean, little girl, and I have better things to do than stand here talking to you."

"No, you don't. You are the murderer of Patrick Stine."

Even I saw the horror in his eyes.

"I ... who are you?"

"I am Ellen Charteris. A very private investigator. The sequence of events is simple but appalling. When Robert Stine found a diamond on a dead colleague, he decided to return it at the first opportunity. That didn't come. He was wounded and sent home. He was still determined that the diamond would be returned. Robert's father, Leonard Stine, found and stole the diamond. After talking about it in at least one public house, and after a small altercation with his son, he was murdered by his brother, Patrick Stine, who stole the diamond. I suspect that you were never far from the diamond, waiting for your chance. After all, you had followed Robert Stine all the way to here from Kurukhstan. When your chance came, you killed Patrick Stine and stole the diamond, with the intention of returning it to the place in your country where it ought to be."

"You are very clever. Yes. I do not know all the details of the first part, but the rest is correct. Now, I must return the diamond."

"And let an innocent man die?"

"People die. The diamond will last forever."

"Only because it is not alive. But I shall remove that temptation and self-justification from you. I promise that the diamond will be returned."

"By whom?"

"By the person who brought it here. The innocent man who is accused of the murder of Leonard Stine. It was his intention before it was stolen from him. It will be his intention when it is returned to him."

From over by the ship, a voice called, "The Eglantine sails on time. All aboard now that's going aboard."

The ship gave a hoot of agreement.

Mr Iqbal turned and looked.

Ellen said, "I will ensure that the diamond is returned. The man who brought here will ensure that it is returned. Your only duty now is to prevent the execution of an innocent man."

Mr Iqbal took a step towards the ship.

"Sailing on time! All aboard!" came the urgent cry.

"Mr Iqbal. Do what is right."

He turned back and said sadly, "I wanted only the diamond. He rushed to protect it, fell and banged his head, and I banged it again, just to be sure that he wouldn't prevent me. That was all. It was not my intention to kill him."

"Tell the policemen that. Tell the truth and leave it with the courts to decide. But now, give

me the diamond and the address of its rightful place."

Ellen was in control.

Mr Iqbal sighed. "Captured by a schoolgirl."

"No. Captured by your conscience."

As Mr Iqbal carefully passed the diamond to her and wrote the address on a piece of paper, I glanced again at the ship. It was then that I noticed Anvil, loitering near the gangplank. Ellen had not relied entirely on the workings of Mr Iqbal's conscience. She was going to have what she wanted, one way or another.

CHAPTER 15

ELLEN CONCLUDES

I sat in the sunshine in the back garden, improving my essay on what I had done during the summer holiday. There were still two weeks to go, but I wanted the task to be more or less finished. Anything worthy of inclusion could be added later. But it wasn't so much a matter of what to put into it as of what to leave out of it. My entire adventure with Ellen would not be included, and that didn't leave much. A visit to relations, the seaside, some visits to the park, and very short diversionary visits to approved places of interest. I hadn't been very interested in anything else. From what I had written so far, it looked as though I had spent the whole summer holiday at the seaside and visiting people and places.

"Hello," called a voice from the back door.

I turned eagerly. I hadn't seen Ellen for three days, and I was missing her. And I wanted some news.

"Well?" I asked when she sat on the grass.

"Your mother has invited me to have a glass of her home-made lemonade. Not another word until I have tasted it."

"You enjoy being mysterious and making me wait for things."

"Of course I do."

I didn't have to wait for long. I detected in my mother's eagerness her desire to keep Ellen and me safely in the garden. Nice and normal and safe. Ellen immediately tried the lemonade and declared it to be excellent. Mother beamed. "There's plenty more," she said.

When Mother had gone back inside, Ellen had another drink, then said, "The police eventually, and somewhat reluctantly, released Robert, who is very grateful to us. It was a considerable blow to their pride to be wrong while I was right. A different detective came to my house to ask me questions about my alleged involvement. It was an unfortunate way of putting it, throwing my parents into immediate panic. Whereas I should have been very willing to give myself a very minor role, in the cause of discretion, I now saw that I must take charge. For the benefit of my parents, and to put him firmly in his place, I explained our careful investigation, detection of the criminal, and our encouragement to him to go to the police station and confess."

Trying not to feel embarrassed, I said, "It's good of you to say 'us' and 'our', but I did very little."

She shook her head. "Jo, in addition to providing valuable support, and companionship, you ask important questions, allowing me to work out the answers. You are my assistant."

"Thank you." What else could I say? Well, I could return to what happened. "What about Iqbal?"

"Complicated. He has confessed to the accidental killing of Patrick Stine, for a diamond whose location he will not reveal, and which, therefore, is not evidence. Without the diamond, his defence would be very weak."

"Where is the diamond?"

"It is on a ship, between here and Kurukhstan, in the safe custody of Robert Stine, who will take the opportunity to slip away and deliver it. I reminded the detective that Patrick Stine had murdered his brother for nothing more than the desire to possess something which had previously been stolen, twice, and that Mr Iqbal was merely attempting to return the diamond to its rightful owner. I suggested to the detective that the return of the diamond and the return of Mr Iqbal might do much to improve relations between our Country and Kurukhstan, thereby saving the lives of many people."

"What did the detective say?"

"He was shocked. He said that justice must run its course, that exceptions couldn't be made, that the law was not something to be manipulated for convenience. I said that I agreed with him. However, I pointed out that just as the lack of the diamond prevented its inclusion as evidence for the benefit of the defence, so it also prevented its inclusion as evidence for the benefit of the prosecution. All that they had was a confession by someone who could produce no evidence and no witnesses. I reminded him again of the probable deaths that would come from further trouble in Kurukhstan, and how they might be avoided by sending this man home."

After a short pause for lemonade, she said, "The detective took the suggestion back to Detective Mellor, he took it to someone higher, and up and up it went, then back down it came, all the way to the Sergeant, who was told to release Mr Iqbal. Constable Harty called and told me what had happened. He said that Detective Mellor is very vexed about the whole thing."

"I'm not surprised. You solved his case and proved that he had arrested the wrong man, and then forced him to release the right man."

"I asked Constable Harty to tell Detective Mellor that I'd be happy to go through the case and explain the different steps. He refused. He seemed to think that it would have a severely detrimental effect on his career prospects."

"Who would disagree?"

"Not anyone who has met Detective Mellor. Constable Harty is our man of common sense, or as near to that as we can reasonably expect. He said that Mr Iqbal had very mixed feelings. He was very pleased to be released, and very grateful to us for our help (I didn't correct her this time.) but it bothered him to have to pay twice for the same journey."

"But much better than being in prison for years."

"Exactly what Constable Harty told him. He agreed. It was just bothering him."

"So, does that mean that everything is all settled?"

"Yes. Mrs Stine continues to work for my parents, and she and her daughter no longer suffer from the tyranny of Leonard Stine. Mary comes with her and helps in her small way. Robert is on his way back to his regiment, and to deliver the diamond. Mr Iqbal will soon be on his way back home. And, I hope, Detective Mellor has learned some valuable lessons."

"More lemonade?" called my mother, already approaching with a large jug. As she added to our glasses, she said, "I shall be popping out for a few minutes. Not far. Poor Miss Sheldon was burgled last night. Some expensive jewellery was stolen. I'll take some cakes and lemonade round to her to cheer her up, poor thing."

I watched Ellen sip her lemonade, and thinking. I said sharply, "Back to school, soon. Back to normal."

"Yes," she said quietly. She called after my mother, "Shall we come, too? Perhaps we can help to cheer her up, too."

"What a nice idea," Mother said. "Best behaviour, of course."

"Of course," said Ellen, and she almost smiled.

The End.

ACKNOWLEDGMENTS

My thanks to fellow author S. S. Saywack for his valuable suggestions.

www.ingramcontent.com/pod-product-compliance
Lightning Source LLC
LaVergne TN
LVHW041115150826
845673LV00007B/2058

* 9 7 8 1 7 3 9 2 1 5 3 8 5 *